circles of care

D1568441

circles of care

Ruth C. Duck

edited by Arthur G. Clyde

The Pilgrim Press
Cleveland, Ohio

The Pilgrim Press, Cleveland, Ohio 44115
© 1998 by The Pilgrim Press

All rights reserved. Published 1998

Printed in the United States of America on acid-free paper

03 02 01 00 99 98 5 4 3 2 1

ISBN 0-8298-1204-0

The Hands of God

The hands of God are work-worn.
Pounding with strong hands
made deft through experience
she kneads the dough,
builds the house,
plants the seed,
the seed that will grow and grow.

The eyes of God are time-worn.
Watching late into the night,
awake before the birds,
she sees all, understands all,
weeps with all,
weeps with tired eyes
and a heart that never closes.

Oh, how experienced she is!
Tell her your secrets.
With massive wisdom
she will listen and probe
till you find the answers
and call them your own.

The eyes of God know your flesh.
She will probe with strong hands,
finding your hurt and tautness,
and leave you sleeping like a child.

Trust her.
She is deep as a cave
and warm as a womb.
Though you may journey far
in strange places,
have adventures stranger still,
her strong, work-worn hands
will welcome you home forever.

By Ruth C. Duck, 1990;
copyright © 1990 by Ruth C. Duck, Evanston, Illinois

CONTENTS

PREFACE

I have called this collection *Circles of Care*, because the phrase "circles of care" keeps showing up in my hymn texts, including "Walls mark our bound'ries" and "In Christ called to worship," as well as a text published elsewhere. The phrase "Christ, stay beside us and embrace the child who dwells within" (in "When painful mem'ries haunt each day") repeats the image in different words. Why does this image attract me so?

A circle is a rich and suggestive image, with particular resonance for women of the past and present, as well as for men. Some years ago, Carole Etzler wrote a song, "We Are Dancing Sarah's Circle," which expressed women's desires to create inclusive circles, rather than to climb hierarchical ladders. When we join hands in a circle, there is always room for one more. When we move in a circle, the leader is still a part of the group. The women's groups in the Methodist church my family attended when I was a child were called circles. Women have joined in knitting circles and sewing circles. Thus, the image of circles evokes memories of shared tasks, talk, laughter, and sometimes tears or conflicts. The Hymnal Development Committee for the *Chalice Hymnal*, on which I served during most of the time when these texts were written, was such a circle of men and women. Its members taught me more about hymn writing and faith than words can say. They were truly a circle of care.

The circle is a symbol of eternity, for it has no beginning or end, and is thus an appropriate symbol for the divine presence in life. Some of the texts, especially the psalm paraphrases, grow out of scripture's testimony to God-with-us; some speak most directly out of contemporary experience. Most relate scripture and experience, but all testify to God's presence in our joy and pain.

My images of circles or surrounding always seem to involve caring, love, or nurture: Circles of care. Several of these hymns grow out of my interest in liturgies of healing in a caring community. The two communion hymns speak of Jesus' open table sharing as a central image of Christian faith. Even the hymns that grow out of painful struggle testify to the care of God, often mediated through caring people. Reading back over the whole collection, I discover that from beginning to end I witness to God's embracing love and to the call to beloved community. And so I track my growth as a Christian and a woman. Though some of these texts sound a call to justice around issues central to feminists (such as reproductive choice, freedom from violence, and alternative imagery for God), my emphasis is on re-creation, not critique of tradition.

A reconstructed church will grow in freedom to use a variety of images about God, both masculine and feminine. At present, we tend to seek gender-inclusiveness hymn by hymn rather than through the whole of a worship service or hymnal. This collection follows a different strategy. Some hymns use only feminine images of God, as a way of complementing the abundance of existing hymns that use masculine images. At least one—"O sons and daughters sing your praise" (a translation of a historic Latin hymn)—uses only masculine images for Jesus Christ. Still other hymns use no gendered imagery (unless one considers the word "God" to be masculine) or use images from both genders. I am seeking to renew imagery for God by speaking in ways that grow out of my life and faith; a discipline of reflecting on my faith experience by writing hymns every Sunday contributes to this. Thus, the images I use vary according to what I want to express. I offer this variety of approaches, sometimes unbalanced in and of themselves, in hopes that along with many other sources, they will help churches recreate the language of worship. I hope that the future church, as a circle of care, will not favor one gender over the other in its language, yet will reflect the freedom of the gospel to use diverse imagery.

The circle of care in a recreated church will embrace far more diversity than we can easily imagine today, and this will be the source of many gifts and much joy and learning. I have caught a glimpse of this future church as, with the encouragement of music editor Arthur Clyde, I sought diversity in musical styles. I am particularly indebted to L. Stanley Davis, a leader in African American, multicultural, and gospel Christian music, for his advice and for his suggestion that I collaborate with Lamont Lenox, a gifted Chicago gospel musician. I appreciate the other talented composers who were willing to provide settings for my texts; they will be described elsewhere in this volume. Special thanks to Arthur Clyde and Kristen Forman for their careful and enthusiastic editorial work.

Others whom I wish to thank include: Robin Knowles Wallace, a Ph.D. graduate from Garrett–Evangelical Theological Seminary presently teaching at the Methodist Theological Seminary in Ohio, who created the indexes and assisted in tune selection; Dori Baker, a present Ph.D. student at Garrett–ETS who provided editorial assistance with the hymn stories; Linda Koops, Administrative Secretary, who prepared correspondence and entered on computer parts of the manuscript; Janice Butz, Dan Damon, Delores Dufner, Kristen Forman, Donna Kasbohm, Al Krass, Lamont Lenox, Joy Patterson, Osvaldo D. Vena, Anita Stauffer, Bobbie Wells-Hargleroad, and Brian Wren, all of whom provided suggestions for improving the texts. Without this circle of caring and talented persons, this book could not have been.

Most of all, I want to give thanks to God for the gift and the call to write hymn texts. Though this work is sometimes a struggle, it is also a joy, above all when my words can be a vehicle for the praise, the lament, and the prayer of the people of God. To God, who encircles us with never-ending care, be all glory.

circles of care

1 God, Our God, Majestic Creator

1 God, our God, ma - jes - tic Cre - a - tor,
2 When I see the work of your fin - gers,
3 Yet you crown our heads, give us hon - or,
4 God, our God, ma - jes - tic Cre - a - tor,
your glo - ry shines be - yond the star - ry skies.
stars shin - ing bright, the time - less moon a - bove,
giv - ing us earth to nur - ture and to keep:
what can we do to thank you for your care?
You si - lence all who scorn your pow'r,
God, who are we that you should care?
all sheep and ox - en, birds that fly,
In youth or age, our lips will sing

WORDS: Free paraphrase of Psalm 8 by Ruth C. Duck, 1996; copyright © 1996 The Pilgrim Press
MUSIC: MAJESTIC CREATOR by Lamont Lenox, 1996; copyright © 1997 The Pilgrim Press

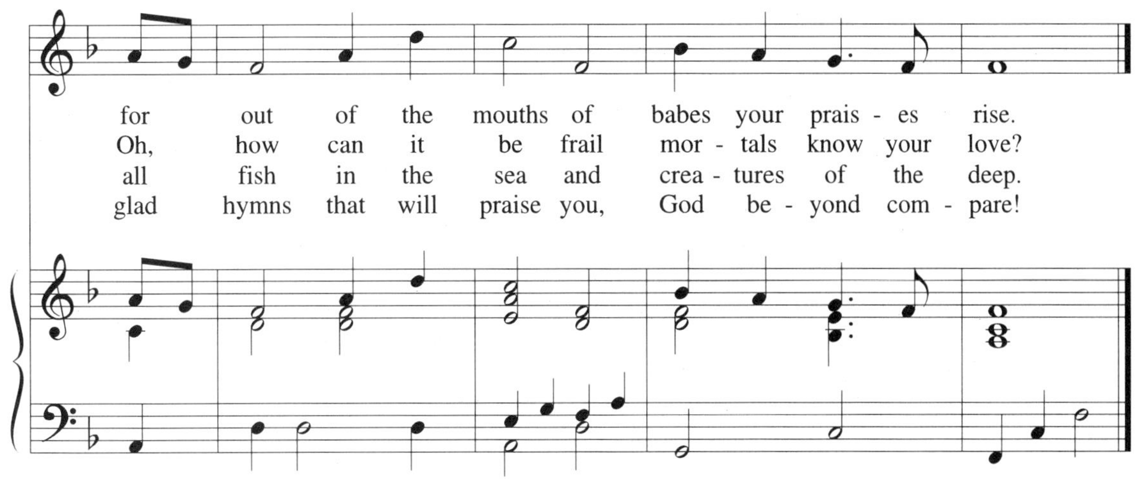
for out of the mouths of babes your prais - es rise.
Oh, how can it be frail mor - tals know your love?
all fish in the sea and crea - tures of the deep.
glad hymns that will praise you, God be - yond com - pare!

1 God, Our God, Majestic Creator

God, our God, majestic Creator,
your glory shines beyond the starry skies.
You silence all who scorn your pow'r,
for out of the mouths of babes your praises rise.

When I see the work of your fingers,
stars shining bright, the timeless moon above,
God, who are we that you should care?
Oh, how can it be frail mortals know your love?

Yet you crown our heads, give us honor,
giving us earth to nurture and to keep:
all sheep and oxen, birds that fly,
all fish in the sea and creatures of the deep.

God, our God, majestic Creator,
what can we do to thank you for your care?
In youth or age, our lips will sing
glad hymns that will praise you, God beyond compare!

WORDS: Free paraphrase of Psalm 8 by Ruth C. Duck, 1996;
copyright © 1996 The Pilgrim Press
METER: 9.10.8.11.

2 Shepherd of My Soul

Not faster than ♩= 76
E♭
Cm
B♭ Cm7 B°
Cm
1 Shep - herd of my soul, you ful - fill my need.
2 When death shades my way, I will fear no ill,
3 You give dai - ly bread near my hun - gry foe.
B♭
E♭
F7
B♭
You have made me whole; I'll go where you lead. You
for by night and day you are with me still. Here
You a - noint my head; bless - ings o - ver - flow. May
Cm D°
E♭
Fm E♭7
A♭
make me a bed where green pas - tures grow. By
your staff and rod com - fort, guard, and guide. Keep
your love and grace ev - er fol - low me. In

Small notes in the accompaniment may be added as the pianist sees fit.

WORDS: Paraphrase of Psalm 23 by Ruth C. Duck, 1996; copyright © 1996 The Pilgrim Press
MUSIC: SOUL SHEPHERD by Lamont Lenox, 1996; copyright © 1997 The Pilgrim Press

E♭ B♭7 E♭ Cm E♭/B♭ B♭ E♭
you I am led where still wa - ters flow.
me, Shep - herd God, safe - ly by your side.
your dwell - ing place may I al - ways be.
Refrain
Fm E♭/G A° G7 E♭/B♭
O Sav - ior, be my guide; lead me all my
E♭ F7 B♭
days, O Shep - herd of my soul.

Cm
D°
E♭
Fm
E♭7/G
Your pres - ence is home, and my joy is your
A♭
E♭
Fm/C
F7
B♭
E♭
praise, O Shep - herd of my soul,
A♭
E♭/B♭
F7
B♭7
E♭
A♭/B♭
O Shep - herd of my soul.
1. E♭
B♭
2. E♭

* For an introduction, begin here.

2 Shepherd of My Soul, You Fulfill My Need

Shepherd of my soul, you fulfill my need.
You have made me whole; I'll go where you lead.
You make me a bed where green pastures grow.
By you I am led where still waters flow.

REFRAIN:
O Savior, be my guide; lead me all my days,
O Shepherd of my soul.
Your presence is home, and my joy is your praise,
O Shepherd of my soul,
O Shepherd of my soul.

When death shades my way, I will fear no ill,
for by night and day you are with me still.
Here your staff and rod comfort, guard, and guide.
Keep me, Shepherd God, safely by your side.
REFRAIN

You give daily bread near my hungry foe.
You anoint my head; blessings overflow.
May your love and grace ever follow me.
In your dwelling place may I always be.
REFRAIN

WORDS: Paraphrase of Psalm 23 by Ruth C. Duck, 1996;
copyright © 1996,The Pilgrim Press
METER: 10.10.10.10. with refrain

3 Wildflowers Bloom and Fade

1 Wild - flow - ers bloom and fade, soon come and gone,
2 Your love will nev - er end; our days are brief.
3 Our lives are like the rose that quick - ly dies.
4 Fill us with faith - ful love as morn - ing wakes.
but God, from age to age you still live on.
Our years are full of sin, lab - or, and grief.
Teach us to count our days; God, make us wise.
Let us re - joice in you as each day breaks.
Old - er than time and space, you are our dwell - ing place.
You turn us back to dust, yet all your ways are just,
Though time flies swift - ly past, God, let our good work last.
May your great work be known, your pow'r on earth be shown.
Keep us in your em- brace, O God, our home.
so we will live in trust, O God, our home.
Your strong arms hold us fast, O God, our home.
Do not for - get your own, O God, our home.

WORDS: Free paraphrase of Psalm 90 by Ruth C. Duck, 1995; copyright © 1996 The Pilgrim Press
MUSIC: INCARNATION by John Bell, 1987; copyright © 1987 by WGRG The Iona Community (Scotland).
Used by permission of G.I.A. Publications, Inc., exclusive agent.

3 Wildflowers Bloom and Fade

Wildflowers bloom and fade,
soon come and gone,
but God, from age to age
you still live on.
Older than time and space,
you are our dwelling place.
Keep us in your embrace,
O God, our home.

Your love will never end;
our days are brief.
Our years are full of sin,
labor, and grief.
You turn us back to dust,
yet all your ways are just,
so we will live in trust,
O God, our home.

Our lives are like the rose
that quickly dies.
Teach us to count our days;
God, make us wise.
Though time flies swiftly past,
God, let our good work last.
Your strong arms hold us fast,
O God, our home.

Fill us with faithful love
as morning wakes.
Let us rejoice in you
as each day breaks.
May your great work be known,
your pow'r on earth be shown.
Do not forget your own,
O God, our home.

WORDS: Free paraphrase of Psalm 90 by Ruth C. Duck, 1995;
copyright © 1996 The Pilgrim Press
METER: 6.4. 6.4. 6.6. 6.4.

4 You Gave My Heart New Songs of Praise

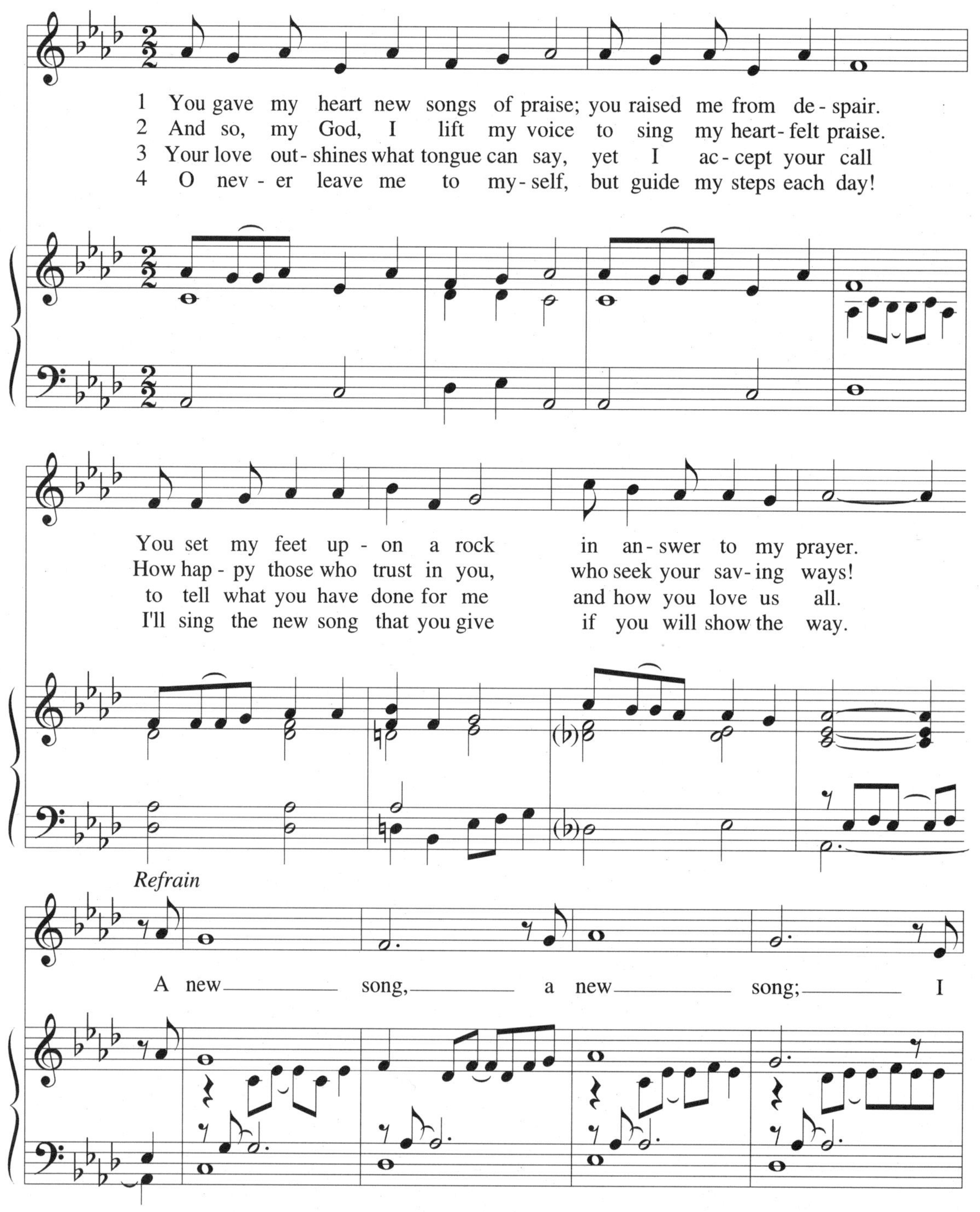
1 You gave my heart new songs of praise; you raised me from de-spair.
2 And so, my God, I lift my voice to sing my heart-felt praise.
3 Your love out-shines what tongue can say, yet I ac-cept your call
4 O nev-er leave me to my-self, but guide my steps each day!
You set my feet up-on a rock in an-swer to my prayer.
How hap-py those who trust in you, who seek your sav-ing ways!
to tell what you have done for me and how you love us all.
I'll sing the new song that you give if you will show the way.
Refrain
A new song, a new song; I

WORDS: Free paraphrase of Psalm 40 by Ruth C. Duck, 1994; copyright © 1996 The Pilgrim Press
MUSIC: NEW SONG by Lamont Lenox, 1996; copyright © 1997 The Pilgrim Press
ALTERNATE TUNE: May be sung to WINCHESTER OLD or AZMON if refrain is omitted.

sing your lov - ing - kind-ness and your grace.
A new song, a
new song, a new song in my
heart, I sing a song of joy and praise.

4 You Gave My Heart New Songs of Praise

You gave my heart new songs of praise;
you raised me from despair.
You set my feet upon a rock
in answer to my prayer.

Refrain:
A new song, a new song:
I sing your loving-kindness and your grace
A new song, a new song,
a new song in my heart,
I sing a song of joy and praise.

And so, my God, I lift my voice
to sing my heartfelt praise.
How happy those who trust in you,
who seek your saving ways!
Refrain

Your love outshines what tongue can say,
yet I accept your call
to tell what you have done for me
and how you love us all.
Refrain

O never leave me to myself,
but guide my steps each day!
I'll sing the new song that you give
if you will show the way.
Refrain

Words: Free paraphrase of Psalm 40 by Ruth C. Duck, 1994;
copyright © 1996 The Pilgrim Press
Meter: 8.6.8.6. (CM) with refrain

5 God Is at Work in Life

♩= 128 - 132
Introduction and interlude before st. 3
With a Swing
1 God is at work in life, re - deem - ing all our loss. No one can sep - a - rate us from the love re - vealed up - on the cross.
2 God is at work in life, to res - cue and re - pair, and nei - ther hard - ship, dan - ger, strife, or sin can keep us from God's care.
3 God is at work in life. Be lift - ed up, my soul! Al - though cre - a - tion suf - fers and de - cays, all shall at last be whole.

WORDS: Ruth C. Duck, 1994; copyright © 1996 The Pilgrim Press
MUSIC: WORKING by Carlton R. Young, 1996; copyright © 1997 The Pilgrim Press

God makes a way a - head when hu - man hope is
Ho - ly the One who builds from hav - oc we re -
God is at work for good in all that we en -
gone. Though tears may last a long and lone - ly
lease, that all cre - a - tion may be rec - on -
dure. We are God's chil - dren through the Spir - it's
night, joy comes at dawn.
ciled, healed, set at peace.
sign. Our hope is sure.
Last time, end.
Last time, end.

5 God Is at Work in Life

God is at work in life,
redeeming all our loss.
No one can separate us from the love
revealed upon the cross.
God makes a way ahead
when human hope is gone.
Though tears may last a long and lonely night,
joy comes at dawn.

God is at work in life
to rescue and repair,
and neither hardship, danger, strife, or sin
can keep us from God's care.
Holy the One who builds
from havoc we release,
that all creation may be reconciled,
healed, set at peace.

God is at work in life.
Be lifted up, my soul!
Although creation suffers and decays,
all shall at last be whole.
God is at work for good
in all that we endure.
We are God's children through the Spirit's sign.
Our hope is sure.

WORDS: Ruth C. Duck, 1994; copyright © 1996 The Pilgrim Press
METER: 6.6.10.6.6.6.10.4.

6 Creator of All Time and Space

GOD OF MANY NAMES

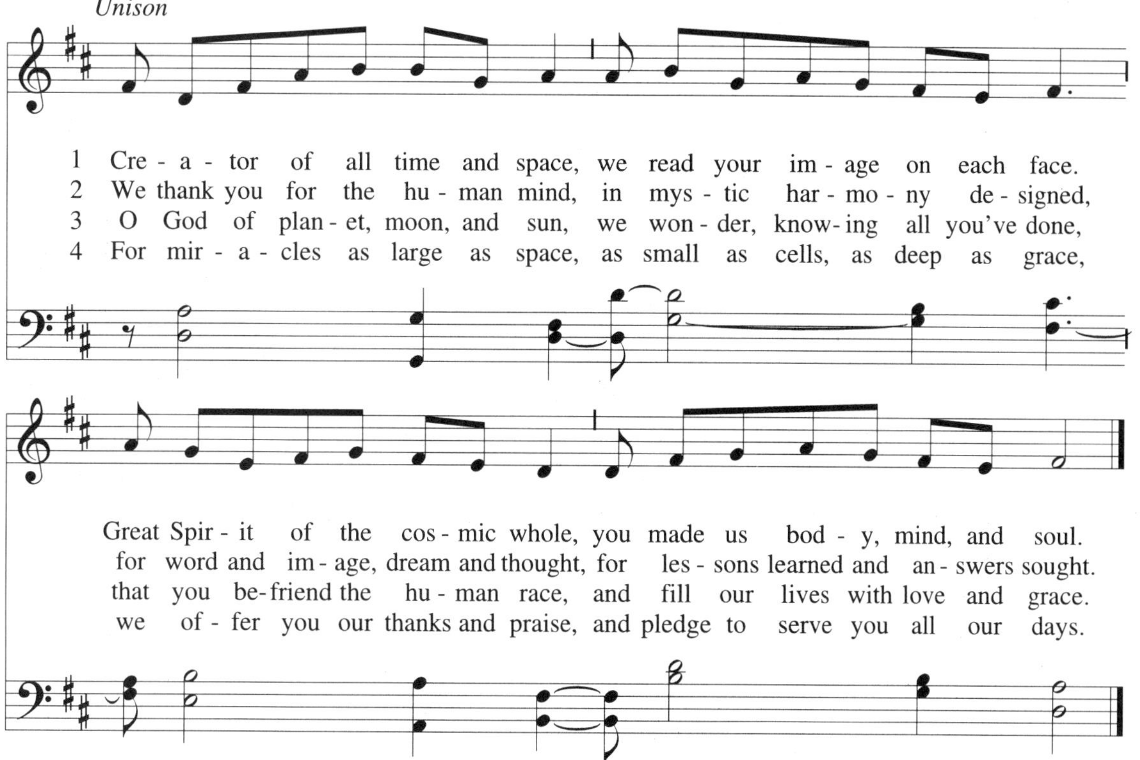
Unison
1 Cre - a - tor of all time and space, we read your im - age on each face.
2 We thank you for the hu - man mind, in mys - tic har - mo - ny de - signed,
3 O God of plan - et, moon, and sun, we won - der, know - ing all you've done,
4 For mir - a - cles as large as space, as small as cells, as deep as grace,
Great Spir - it of the cos - mic whole, you made us bod - y, mind, and soul.
for word and im - age, dream and thought, for les - sons learned and an - swers sought.
that you be - friend the hu - man race, and fill our lives with love and grace.
we of - fer you our thanks and praise, and pledge to serve you all our days.

WORDS: Ruth C. Duck, 1993; copyright © 1996 The Pilgrim Press
MUSIC: CONDITOR ALME SIDERUM, ancient Sarum plainsong, Mode IV;
harm., *The New Century Hymnal,* 1994; copyright © 1994 The Pilgrim Press
ALTERNATE TUNE: TALLIS' CANON

6 Creator of All Time and Space

Creator of all time and space,
we read your image on each face.
Great Spirit of the cosmic whole,
you made us body, mind, and soul.

We thank you for the human mind,
in mystic harmony designed,
for word and image, dream and thought,
for lessons learned and answers sought.

O God of planet, moon, and sun,
we wonder, knowing all you've done,
that you befriend the human race,
and fill our lives with love and grace.

For miracles as large as space,
as small as cells, as deep as grace,
we offer you our thanks and praise,
and pledge to serve you all our days.

WORDS: Ruth C. Duck, 1993; copyright © 1996 The Pilgrim Press
METER: 8.8.8.8. (LM)

7 Come and Seek the Ways of Wisdom

1 Come and seek the ways of Wis - dom, she who danced when
2 Lis - ten to the voice of Wis - dom, cry - ing in the
3 Sis - ter Wis - dom, come, as - sist us; nur - ture all who
earth was new. Fol - low close - ly what she teach - es,
mar - ket - place. Hear the Word made flesh a - mong us,
seek re - birth. Spir - it - guide and close com - pan - ion,
for her words are right and true. Wis - dom clears the
full of glo - ry, truth, and grace. When the word takes
bring to light our sa - cred worth. Free us to be -

WORDS: Ruth C. Duck, 1993; copyright © 1996 The Pilgrim Press
MUSIC: MADELEINE by Donna Kasbohm, 1995; copyright © 1997 The Pilgrim Press
ALTERNATE TUNE: PICARDY

path to jus - tice, show - ing us what love must do.
root and rip - ens, peace and righ - teous - ness em - brace.
come your peo - ple, ho - ly friends of God and earth.

7 Come and Seek the Ways of Wisdom

Come and seek the ways of Wisdom,
she who danced when earth was new.
Follow closely what she teaches,
for her words are right and true.
Wisdom clears the path to justice,
showing us what love must do.

Listen to the voice of Wisdom,
crying in the marketplace.
Hear the Word made flesh among us,
full of glory, truth, and grace.
When the word takes root and ripens,
peace and righteousness embrace.

Sister Wisdom, come, assist us;
nurture all who seek rebirth.
Spirit-guide and close companion,
bring to light our sacred worth.
Free us to become your people,
holy friends of God and earth.

Words: Ruth C. Duck, 1993; copyright © 1996 The Pilgrim Press
Meter: 8.7.8.7.8.7.

8 Like a Pleading Widow

1 Like a plead - ing wid - ow, God, you press for right,
2 Like a hound of heav - en you pur - sue us all.
3 "Oh, how long, my peo - ple, will you run a - way?
cry - ing out for jus - tice, call - ing day and night. Screened in flash - ing im - age,
Tire - less in your seek - ing, cease - less in your call. Though we draw a cir - cle
When will you do jus - tice? Will you still de - lay?" God, we hear you speak - ing;
beg - ging on the street, God, you nev - er leave us. Ev' - ry day we meet.
meant to keep you out, you, in love, en - com - pass way - ward fear and doubt.
help us turn a - round, so that when you call us, just - ice may be found.

Words: Ruth C. Duck, 1995; copyright © 1996 The Pilgrim Press
Music: HOPKINS by Donna Kasbohm, 1996; copyright © 1997 The Pilgrim Press
Alternate Tune: CRANHAM

8 Like a Pleading Widow

Like a pleading widow,
God, you press for right,
crying out for justice,
calling day and night.
Screened in flashing image,
begging on the street,
God, you never leave us.
Ev'ry day we meet.

Like a hound of heaven
you pursue us all.
Tireless in your seeking,
ceaseless in your call.
Though we draw a circle
meant to keep you out,
you, in love, encompass
wayward fear and doubt.

"Oh, how long, my people,
will you run away?
When will you do justice?
Will you still delay?"
God, we hear you speaking;
help us turn around,
so that when you call us,
justice may be found.

WORDS: Ruth C. Duck, 1995; copyright © 1996 The Pilgrim Press
METER: 6.5.6.5.D

9 Take My Yoke upon You

Unison
1 Take my yoke up - on you, all who la - bor long.
2 Come a - way, dis - cip - le; come, re - treat a while.
3 Trust - ing and re - turn - ing, you shall grow in strength.
4 When your world is chang - ing at a breath - less pace,
5 When the night grows long - er, and the end is near,
I am al - ways with you. Learn my way of liv - ing,
I will trav - el with you, bless - ing des - ert plac - es,
I am al - ways with you; since my love de - signed you,
I am al - ways pres - ent, cen - ter in life's turn - ing,
I am your com - pan - ion, hope in joy or sor - row,
sim - ple and for - giv - ing, and I will give you rest.
fill - ing sab - bath spac - es, and I will give you rest.
seek and I will find you, and I will give you rest.
light in la - bor's learn - ing, and I will give you rest.
home be - yond to - mor - row, and I will give you rest.

WORDS: Ruth C. Duck, 1995; copyright © 1996 The Pilgrim Press
MUSIC: TACOMA by Daniel Charles Damon, 1995; copyright © 1996 Hope Publishing Co., Carol Stream, IL 60188. All rights reserved. Used by permission.

9 Take My Yoke upon You

Take my yoke upon you,
all who labor long.
I am always with you.
Learn my way of living,
simple and forgiving,
and I will give you rest.

Come away, disciple;
come, retreat a while.
I will travel with you,
blessing desert places,
filling sabbath spaces,
and I will give you rest.

Trusting and returning,
you shall grow in strength.
I am always with you;
since my love designed you,
seek and I will find you,
and I will give you rest.

When your world is changing
at a breathless pace,
I am always present,
center in life's turning,
light in labor's learning,
and I will give you rest.

When the night grows longer,
and the end is near,
I am your companion,
hope in joy or sorrow,
home beyond tomorrow,
and I will give you rest.

Words: Ruth C. Duck, 1995; copyright © 1996 The Pilgrim Press
Meter: 6.5.6.6.6.6.

10 Spirit, Open My Heart

Chorus
F Bb F Bb
Spir - it, o - pen my heart to the joy and
C Dm Bb F/C
pain of liv - ing. As you love may I
Dm F/C Gm F/A Bb
love, in re - ceiv - ing and in giv - ing,
C7 F Bb F
Last time, end here.
Spir - it, o - pen my heart.
F Bb F F/A
1 God, re - place my ston - y heart with a
2 Write your love up - on my heart as my
3 May I weep with those who weep, share the

WORDS: Ruth C. Duck, 1994; copyright © 1996 The Pilgrim Press
MUSIC: WILD MOUNTAIN THYME, Irish traditional melody; arr. Arthur G. Clyde, 1997; copyright © 1997 The Pilgrim Press

B♭ C Dm Dmin7 Gm/B♭ F/C
heart that's kind and ten-der. All my cold - ness and
law, my goal, my sto - ry. In each thought, word, and
joy of sis - ter, broth-er. In the wel - come of
Dm F/C Gm F/A B♭ C
fear to your grace I now sur - ren - der.
deed, may my liv - ing bring you glo - ry.
Christ, may we wel - come one an - oth - er.

10 Spirit, Open My Heart

REFRAIN:
Spirit, open my heart
to the joy and pain of living.
As you love may I love,
in receiving and in giving.
Spirit, open my heart.

God, replace my stony heart
with a heart that's kind and tender.
All my coldness and fear
to your grace I now surrender.
REFRAIN

Write your love upon my heart
as my law, my goal, my story.
In each thought, word, and deed,
may my living bring you glory.
REFRAIN

May I weep with those who weep,
share the joy of sister, brother.
In the welcome of Christ,
may we welcome one another.
REFRAIN

WORDS: Ruth C. Duck, 1994; copyright © 1996 The Pilgrim Press
METER: 7.8.6.8. with refrain

11 God of Wisdom, God of Grace

1 God of wis - dom, God of grace, na - ture tells your sto - ry,
2 Word em - bod - ied, word of life, light of ev' - ry na - tion,
3 Spir - it, lift the veils of fear that ob - scure our know - ing.
and in Je - sus' lov - ing face you re - flect your glo - ry.
you have en - tered hu - man strife, show - ing right re - la - tion.
Let the Glo - rious Sun ap - pear that will aid our grow - ing.
Je - sus Christ, your child most dear, mir - rors you, life's foun - tain,
Friend of out - casts, claim our hearts by your peace and pas - sion;
Change us slow - ly day by day by your grace per - fect - ing.
as a lake both calm and clear mir - rors tree and moun - tain.
may our lives, our work, our arts, mir - ror your com - pas - sion.
May our lives, though formed of clay, shine, your light re - flect - ing.

WORDS: Ruth C. Duck, 1994; copyright © 1996 The Pilgrim Press
MUSIC: ST. KEVIN by Arthur S. Sullivan, 1872

11 God of Wisdom, God of Grace

God of wisdom, God of grace,
nature tells your story,
and in Jesus' loving face
you reflect your glory.
Jesus Christ, your child most dear,
mirrors you, life's fountain,
as a lake both calm and clear
mirrors tree and mountain.

Word embodied, word of life,
light of ev'ry nation,
you have entered human strife,
showing right relation.
Friend of outcasts, claim our hearts
by your peace and passion;
may our lives, our work, our arts,
mirror your compassion.

Spirit, lift the veils of fear
that obscure our knowing.
Let the Glorious Sun appear
that will aid our growing.
Change us slowly day by day
by your grace perfecting.
May our lives, though formed of clay,
shine, your light reflecting.

Words: Ruth C. Duck, 1996; copyright © 1996 The Pilgrim Press
Meter: 7.6.7.6.D

12 In the Dawn of the Ages

Unison
1 In the dawn of the a - ges God cre - a - ted the earth. Ev' - ry
2 In the dew of the morn - ing with her work al - most done, the Cre -
3 So she reached down and gath - ered up the clay in her hand, and she
liv - ing crea - ture found in God its birth, from the birds in the sky to the
a - tor said at ris - ing of the sun, "On - ly one thing is lack - ing from
shaped and formed a wom - an and a man. Then she breathed in - to each her own
deer in the wood. She looked all a - round and she said, "It is good."
earth far and wide: the chil - dren of earth liv - ing here by my side."
life - giv - ing soul. She gave each a long - ing to love and be whole.
Chorus
One God, Cre - a - tor of us all, in you we find our life and call. Great
Spir - it and source of birth, we praise your name in all the earth.
Last time, end here.

WORDS: Ruth C. Duck, 1974, rev. 1996; copyright © 1996 The Pilgrim Press
MUSIC: SIMPLE GIFTS, Shaker melody, 19th century; arr. Arthur G. Clyde, 1997;
copyright © 1997 The Pilgrim Press

12 In the Dawn of the Ages

In the dawn of the ages God created the earth.
Ev'ry living creature found in God its birth,
from the birds in the sky to the deer in the wood.
She looked all around and she said, "It is good."

Refrain:
One God, Creator of us all,
in you we find our life and call.
Great Spirit and source of birth,
we praise your name in all the earth.

In the dew of the morning with her work almost done,
the Creator said at rising of the sun,
"Only one thing is lacking from earth far and wide:
the children of earth living here by my side."
Refrain

So she reached down and gathered up the clay
in her hand,
and she shaped and formed a woman and a man.
Then she breathed into each her own life-giving soul.
She gave each a longing to love and be whole.
Refrain

Words: Ruth C. Duck, 1974, revised 1996; copyright © 1996
The Pilgrim Press
Meter: 13.11.12.11. with refrain

13 Your Glory, O God

♩ = 116
Unison
1 Your glo - ry, O God, in Christ is dis - played,
2 The gos - pel of Christ shines deep in our hearts,
3 Trans - form us, O God; by grace may we be
the glo - ry you dream for all you have made,
il - lu - mines our work, our wor - ship and arts.
re - flec - tions of Christ in grow - ing de - gree.
for Christ bears your im - print and mir - rors your face,
In - spired by your Spir - it, who frees us from fear,
Re - move ev - ery tar - nish that dims your de - sign;

* May be sung a half-step higher.

WORDS: Ruth C. Duck, 1996; copyright © 1996 The Pilgrim Press
MUSIC: GOD'S IMAGE by Carlton R. Young, 1996; copyright © 1997 The Pilgrim Press
ALTERNATE TUNE: HANOVER

re - flect - ing your im - age, your wis - dom and grace.
we pray that our like - ness to Christ may be clear.
like Christ, may we mir - ror your glo - ry di - vine.

13 Your Glory, O God

Your glory, O God, in Christ is displayed,
the glory you dream for all you have made,
for Christ bears your imprint and mirrors your face,
reflecting your image, your wisdom and grace.

The gospel of Christ shines deep in our hearts,
illumines our work, our worship and arts.
Inspired by your Spirit, who frees us from fear,
we pray that our likeness to Christ may be clear.

Transform us, O God; by grace may we be
reflections of Christ in growing degree.
Remove every tarnish that dims your design;
like Christ, may we mirror your glory divine.

WORDS: Ruth C. Duck, 1996; copyright © 1996 The Pilgrim Press
METER: 10.10.11.11.

14 Glory to God, and Peace on Earth!

1 Glo - ry to God, and peace on earth! We wor - ship and bless the God of our birth! Thanks - giv - ing and
2 O Lamb of God, we praise your name, for you take a - way the world's sin and shame. O Christ, give us
3 Spir - it of God, we sing to you. O Giv - er of life, your touch makes us new. Come breathe on us

WORDS: Free paraphrase of the Gloria in Excelsis by Ruth C. Duck, 1996;
copyright © 1996 The Pilgrim Press
MUSIC: JOYFUL VOICES by Lamont Lenox, 1996; copyright © 1997 The Pilgrim Press

praise, be yours, God most high. You are the Ho - ly One.
peace, and grant us your care. Je - sus, the Lamb of God,
now; trans - form all our ways. O Spir - it, stay with us,
Your glo - ry fills the sky.
bend down and hear our prayer.
and fill our hearts with praise.
1., 2.
3.

14 Glory to God, and Peace on Earth!

Glory to God, and peace on earth!
We worship and bless the God of our birth!
Thanksgiving and praise, be yours, God most high.
You are the Holy One.
Your glory fills the sky.

O Lamb of God, we praise your name,
for you take away the world's sin and shame.
O Christ, give us peace, and grant us your care.
Jesus, the Lamb of God,
bend down and hear our prayer.

Spirit of God, we sing to you.
O Giver of life, your touch makes us new.
Come breathe on us now; transform all our ways.
O Spirit, stay with us,
and fill our hearts with praise.

WORDS: Ruth C. Duck, 1996 (free paraphrase of the Gloria in Excelsis); copyright © 1996 The Pilgrim Press
METER: 8.10.10.6.6.

15 We Thank You, God, for Prayer

GOD OF MANY NAMES

1 We thank you, God, for prayer, the pres - ent gift of grace,
2 What moth - er will de - sert the child that she has borne?
3 What fa - ther will give stone when chil - dren ask for food?
4 O Spir - it, lin - ger here to guide us night and day.
the fount of your un - fail - ing care for all who seek your face.
You will not leave the lost and hurt for - got - ten or for - lorn.
A great - er gift you give your own— the Spir - it of all good.
Come, free us from our stub - born fear and teach us how to pray.

WORDS: Ruth C. Duck, 1994; copyright © 1996 The Pilgrim Press
MUSIC: TAFT STREET by Brent Stratten, 1993; copyright © 1995 The Chalice Press
ALTERNATE TUNE: BOYLSTON

15 We Thank You, God, for Prayer

We thank you, God, for prayer,
the present gift of grace,
the fount of your unfailing care
for all who seek your face.

What mother will desert
the child that she has borne?
You will not leave the lost and hurt
forgotten or forlorn.

What father will give stone
when children ask for food?
A greater gift you give your own—
the Spirit of all good.

O Spirit, linger here
to guide us night and day.
Come, free us from our stubborn fear
and teach us how to pray.

WORDS: Ruth C. Duck, 1994; copyright ©1996 The Pilgrim Press
METER: 6.6.8.6. (SM)

16 Blessed Darkness

Unison
Refrain
D A Bmin G D Bmin C A
Bless-ed dark-ness, bless the dark-ness where God makes the spir-it whole.
D A F♯ Bmin F♯min Emin A7 D
Last time end here.
Bear-ing birth and new be-gin-nings comes the dark night of the soul.
Last time end here.
Bmin F♯min G C♯dim F♯min Bmin Emin G A
1 Though we love our well-lit high-ways, as we rush from place to place,
2 When we live in faith, not know-ing what ho-ri-zon lies a-head,
3 God, the lov-ing gard'-ner, tends us, as in dark soil life un-folds.
Emin D A D F♯min A D E A
for-est trails through shad-ed by-ways of-fer great-er gifts of grace.
clouds ap-pear to guide our go-ing; God gives man-na, dai-ly bread.
Like a mid-wife, God be-friends us, wel-comes life the dark womb holds.

WORDS: Ruth C. Duck, 1996; copyright © 1996 The Pilgrim Press
MUSIC: BLESSED DARKNESS by Ruth C. Duck, 1996; copyright © 1997 The Pilgrim Press
ALTERNATE TUNE: IN BABILONE

16 Blessed Darkness

Refrain:
Blessed darkness, bless the darkness
where God makes the spirit whole.
Bearing birth and new beginnings
comes the dark night of the soul.

Though we love our well-lit highways,
as we rush from place to place,
forest trails through shaded byways
offer greater gifts of grace.
Refrain

When we live in faith, not knowing
what horizon lies ahead,
clouds appear to guide our going;
God gives manna, daily bread.
Refrain

God, the loving gard'ner, tends us,
as in dark soil life unfolds.
Like a midwife, God befriends us,
welcomes life the dark womb holds.
Refrain

Words: Ruth C. Duck, 1996; copyright © 1996 The Pilgrim Press
Meter: 8.7.8.7.D (or 8.7.8.7. with refrain)

17 I Reflect the Image of the Maker

1 I re - flect the im - age of the Mak - er, spark of all cre - a - tive flame, she who is and al - ways will be. Praise her name! Praise her name!
2 I re - flect the im - age of the Chris - ta, love em - bod - ied on the earth, she who calls the world to jus - tice. Praise her worth! Praise her worth!
3 I re - flect the im - age of the Spir - it, breath and wind who blows us free, she who gent - ly guides our jour - ney. Prais - es be! Prais - es be!
1-2
3

WORDS: Ruth C. Duck, 1993; copyright © 1996 The Pilgrim Press
MUSIC: WISDOM WAYS by Donna Kasbohm, 1996; copyright © 1997 The Pilgrim Press

17 I Reflect the Image of the Maker

I reflect the image of the Maker,
spark of all creative flame,
she who is and always will be.
Praise her name! Praise her name!

I reflect the image of the Christa,
love embodied on the earth,
she who calls the world to justice.
Praise her worth! Praise her worth!

I reflect the image of the Spirit,
breath and wind who blows us free,
she who gently guides our journey.
Praises be! Praises be!

Words: Ruth C. Duck, 1993; copyright © 1996 The Pilgrim Press
Meter: 10.7.8.6.

18 We Thank You, God, for Sunday

1 We thank you, God, for Sun - day, the day when Christ a - rose,
2 The first day of cre - a - tion when naught had come to be,
3 This first day as we gath - er we seek new life, new birth:
the day of praise and meet - ing, of bles - sing and re - pose.
your Ho - ly Spir - it brood - ed up - on the form - less sea.
the eighth day of cre - a - tion when you re - new the earth.
Each day, each hour is sa - cred; you guide us all the way.
And then you split the si - lence and spoke: "Let there be light!"
Re - mold your yearn - ing peo - ple; re - shape our shat - tered clay;
We praise you most for Sun - day, our res - ur - rec - tion day.
Be - fore the dusk of eve - ning you made both day and night.
so may we rise each morn - ing to res - ur - rec - tion day.

WORDS: Ruth C. Duck, 1996; copyright © 1996 The Pilgrim Press
MUSIC: MUNICH, *Neuvermehrtes Gesangbuch,* Meinningen, 1693
ALTERNATE TUNE: MEIRIONYDD

18 We Thank You, God, for Sunday

We thank you, God, for Sunday,
the day when Christ arose,
the day of praise and meeting,
of blessing and repose.
Each day, each hour is sacred;
you guide us all the way.
We praise you most for Sunday,
our resurrection day.

The first day of creation
when naught had come to be,
your Holy Spirit brooded
upon the formless sea.
And then you split the silence
and spoke: "Let there be light!"
Before the dusk of evening
you made both day and night.

This first day as we gather
we seek new life, new birth:
the eighth day of creation
when you renew the earth.
Remold your yearning people;
reshape our shattered clay;
so may we rise each morning
to resurrection day.

Words: Ruth C. Duck, 1996; copyright © 1996 The Pilgrim Press
Meter: 7.6.7.6.D

19 Here at Jordan's River

1 Here at Jor - dan's riv - er all is washed a - way.
2 We at Jor - dan's riv - er meet on lev - el ground.
3 God, re - form, re - new us; turn us toward your will.
As God's reign draws near - er, noth - ing is the same.
Val - leys are up - lift - ed; moun - tains fall to earth.
Till our hearts for learn - ing; root us in your word.
Gone are class and sta - tus; gone, de - grees and fame.
None dare trust their lin - eage; none need doubt their worth.
May the fruits of ac - tion grow from all we've heard.
Grace a - lone can save us on God's judg - ment day.
Still the pro - phet asks us, "Will you turn a - round?"
As we lose our old lives, God, be with us still.

WORDS: Ruth C. Duck, 1995; copyright © 1996 The Pilgrim Press
MUSIC: NOEL NOUVELET, French carol, 15th century; harm. Arthur G. Clyde, 1997; copyright © 1997 The Pilgrim Press
ALTERNATE TUNE: KING'S WESTON

19 Here at Jordan's River

Here at Jordan's river
all is washed away.
As God's reign draws nearer,
nothing is the same.
Gone are class and status;
gone, degrees and fame.
Grace alone can save us
on God's judgment day.

We at Jordan's river
meet on level ground.
Valleys are uplifted;
mountains fall to earth.
None dare trust their lineage;
none need doubt their worth.
Still the prophet asks us,
"Will you turn around?"

God, reform, renew us;
turn us toward your will.
Till our hearts for learning;
root us in your word.
May the fruits of action
grow from all we've heard.
As we lose our old lives,
God, be with us still.

Words: Ruth C. Duck, 1995; copyright © 1996 The Pilgrim Press
Meter: 6.5.6.5.D

20 You Shall Draw with Gladness

1 You shall draw with glad - ness from the wells of grace.
2 Love di - vine sur - pass - es loves we hold most dear.
3 Bring - ing fire in win - ter, Je - sus comes to save,
Though your years have long been dry, you shall see God's face.
God is great - er than our guilt, strong - er than our fear.
pour - ing out the Spir - it's pow'r, o - pen - ing the grave.
Child of God, be joy - ful; no more shall you mourn.
Child of God, be joy - ful; wait and watch and pray.
Child of God, be joy - ful! God is draw - ing near.
God will not de - sert you, child whom she has borne.
Streams shall wash the des - ert as God clears the way.
Grace springs forth a - mong us, flow - ing fresh and clear.

WORDS: Ruth C. Duck, 1994; copyright © 1996 The Pilgrim Press
MUSIC: CRANHAM by Gustav Holst, 1906
ALTERNATE TUNE: ADORO TE DEVOTE

20 You Shall Draw with Gladness

You shall draw with gladness
from the wells of grace.
Though your years have long been dry,
you shall see God's face.
Child of God, be joyful;
no more shall you mourn.
God will not desert you,
child whom she has borne.

Love divine surpasses
loves we hold most dear.
God is greater than our guilt,
stronger than our fear.
Child of God, be joyful;
wait and watch and pray.
Streams shall wash the desert
as God clears the way.

Bringing fire in winter,
Jesus comes to save,
pouring out the Spirit's pow'r,
opening the grave.
Child of God, be joyful!
God is drawing near.
Grace springs forth among us,
flowing fresh and clear.

Words: Ruth C. Duck, 1994; copyright © 1996 The Pilgrim Press
Meter: 6.5.7.5.6.5.6.5.

21 O Word Made Flesh among Us

G D G C D7 G
1 O Word made flesh a - mong us, you bless the world we know;
2 O Child of cross and man - ger, both hu - man and di - vine,
3 And - won - der of all won - ders! - though we are formed of earth,
G D G C D7 G
the sheep, the straw, the sta - ble; the rose, the spark - ling snow.
you know our flesh, our na - ture, our need for sense and sign.
you call us God's own chil - dren, re - born by Spir - it's birth.
G D C Am7 D
True God, yet born of Mar - y, you share our joy and loss.
And so you come to meet us, all full of truth and grace.
O Word of God, we greet you with grate - ful hymns of praise,
G D G C D7 G
The wood that shapes your cra - dle one day will form a cross.
You make the com - mon ho - ly: our world, our time, our space.
for you re - veal the sa - cred that weaves through all our days.

WORDS: Ruth C. Duck, 1996; copyright © 1996 The Pilgrim Press
MUSIC: BRED DINA VIDA VINGAR, Swedish folk tune; harm. Arthur G. Clyde, 1997;
copyright © 1997 The Pilgrim Press

21 O Word Made Flesh among Us

O Word made flesh among us,
you bless the world we know;
the sheep, the straw, the stable;
the rose, the sparkling snow.
True God, yet born of Mary,
you share our joy and loss.
The wood that shapes your cradle
one day will form a cross.

O Child of cross and manger,
both human and divine,
you know our flesh, our nature,
our need for sense and sign.
And so you come to meet us,
all full of truth and grace.
You make the common holy:
our world, our time, our space.

And–wonder of all wonders!–
though we are formed of earth,
you call us God's own children,
reborn by Spirit's birth.
O Word of God, we greet you
with grateful hymns of praise,
for you reveal the sacred
that weaves through all our days.

WORDS: Ruth C. Duck, 1996; copyright © 1996 The Pilgrim Press
METER: 7.6.7.6.D

22 Not in Grand Estate

G
G7
C
CMaj7
1 Not in grand es - tate, you make your earth - ly home.
2 Not for just the wise, you come to bring good news.
3 Not by hum - an will, but by the Spir - it's pow'r,
D
D
Em
Not a - mong the great, you come to bring shal - om.
Those the rich de - spise are peo - ple whom you choose.
you are with us still to help us in this hour.
G
G7
C
CMaj7
Liv - ing with the poor, you shine with God's own light.
Sag - es from a - far and shep - herds sing your birth.
Com - ing in God's name to set all peo - ple free,
D
D
Em
D
Knock u - pon our door; find shel - ter for the night.
Show us by your star your pres - ence here on earth.
Je - sus, you pro - claim the year of ju - bi - lee.

WORDS: Ruth C. Duck, 1997; copyright © 1997 The Pilgrim Press
MUSIC: GARRETT by Osvaldo D. Vena, 1997; copyright © 1997 The Pilgrim Press

Refrain
G
D
Em
G7
Je - sus, show the way; your liv - ing word has
C
D
G
D
freed us. Come and shine to - day.
G
D
Em
G7
Je - sus, show the way, and
C
D
G
send your star to lead us.

22 Not in Grand Estate

Not in grand estate,
you make your earthly home.
Not among the great,
you come to bring shalom.
Living with the poor,
you shine with God's own light.
Knock upon our door;
find shelter for the night.

Refrain:
Jesus, show the way;
your loving word has freed us.
Come and shine today.
Jesus, show the way,
and send your star to lead us.

Not for just the wise,
you come to bring good news.
Those the rich despise
are people whom you choose.
Sages from afar
and shepherds sing your birth.
Show us by your star
your presence here on earth.
Refrain

Not by human will,
but by the Spirit's pow'r,
you are with us still
to help us in this hour.
Coming in God's name
to set all people free,
Jesus, you proclaim
the year of jubilee.
Refrain

Words: Ruth C. Duck, 1997; copyright © 1997 The Pilgrim Press
Meter: 5.6.5.6.5.6. with refrain

23 When Mary Bathed Our Savior's Feet

Unison
1 When Mar - y bathed our Sav - ior's feet, she
2 Since Je - sus knew his time had come, he
3 But Pe - ter said when Je - sus knelt, "No!
4 And we— have we no sign to show con -
5 As Christ has loved us, let us love in
cared for him in grief, but Ju - das grum - bled
called his friends to meet, and, pour - ing wa - ter
this shall nev - er be." Christ said, "Un - less I
cern for those who grieve? When love is of - fered,
touch, in act, in sign. In giv - ing and re -
at the waste be - cause he was a thief.
in a bowl, be - gan to wash their feet.
wash your feet, you have no part in me."
are we slow to o - pen and re - ceive?
ceiv - ing care we share in life di - vine.

WORDS: Ruth C. Duck, 1995; copyright © 1996 The Pilgrim Press
MUSIC: RUTH by Brent Stratten, 1995; copyright © 1997 The Pilgrim Press
ALTERNATE TUNE: ST. FLAVIAN

23 When Mary Bathed Our Savior's Feet

When Mary bathed our Savior's feet,
she cared for him in grief,
but Judas grumbled at the waste
because he was a thief.

Since Jesus knew his time had come,
he called his friends to meet,
and, pouring water in a bowl,
began to wash their feet.

But Peter said when Jesus knelt,
"No! this shall never be."
Christ said, "Unless I wash your feet,
you have no part in me."

And we—have we no sign to show
concern for those who grieve?
When love is offered, are we slow
to open and receive?

As Christ has loved us, let us love
in touch, in act, in sign.
In giving and receiving care
we share in life divine.

Words: Ruth C. Duck, 1995, copyright © 1996 The Pilgrim Press
Meter: 8.6.8.6. (CM)

24 How Could a God Whose Name Is Love

1 How could a God whose name is love seek blood to pay sin's price?
2 Did Je - sus come as God's own child to share each hu - man tear?
3 In Je - sus Christ we meet a God whose love em - brac - es all,
Are tor - ture, shame, and sense - less death a ho - ly sac - ri - fice?
Did Je - sus die in speak - ing truth that ru - lers will not hear?
who weeps when chil - dren are a - bused, who hears each spar - row fall.
Each vi - o - lent crime is trag - ic loss; how could it be God's will?
If Wis - dom hangs up - on a tree, what, then, are we to do?
When grace is an - cient as the earth, we need not wor - ship death.
How can we glo - ri - fy the cross when vic - tims suf - fer still?
Must we, like Je - sus, risk our lives for what is just and true?
So let us live in ten - der care for all whom Love gives breath.

WORDS: Ruth C. Duck, 1993; copyright © 1996 The Pilgrim Press
MUSIC: TALLIS' THIRD TUNE by Thomas Tallis, c. 1557
ALTERNATE TUNE: KINGSFOLD

24 How Could a God Whose Name Is Love

How could a God whose name is love
seek blood to pay sin's price?
Are torture, shame, and senseless death
a holy sacrifice?
Each violent crime is tragic loss;
how could it be God's will?
How can we glorify the cross
when victims suffer still?

Did Jesus come as God's own child
to share each human tear?
Did Jesus die in speaking truth
that rulers will not hear?
If Wisdom hangs upon a tree,
what, then, are we to do?
Must we, like Jesus, risk our lives
for what is just and true?

In Jesus Christ we meet a God
whose love embraces all,
who weeps when children are abused,
who hears each sparrow fall.
When grace is ancient as the earth,
we need not worship death.
So let us live in tender care
for all whom Love gives breath.

Words: Ruth C. Duck, 1993; copyright © 1996 The Pilgrim Press
Meter: 8.6.8.6.D (CMD)

25 O Sons and Daughters, Sing Your Praise

Antiphon (may be sung at beginning and end)

Al - le - lu - ia! Al - le - lu- ia! Al - le - lu- ia! Al - le - lu - ia!
1,7 O sons and daugh - ters, sing your praise on this most ho - ly
2 When Mag - da - lene and Sa - lo - me and Mar - y went where
3 An an - gel greet - ed them and said, "The Christ is ris - en
4 A - mong dis - cip - les Christ ap - peared. "My peace be with you,"
5 "Come, Thom - as, see my hands and side. I am the one they
6 "How blest are those who do not see yet place their faith and
day of days. For Christ from death to life is raised.
Je - sus lay, they found the stone was rolled a - way.
from the dead. To Gal - i - lee he goes a - head."
was his word, but Thom - as doubt - ed when he heard.
cru - ci - fied." "My God, my Sav - ior!" Tho - mas cried.
trust in me. They shall have life e - ter - nal - ly."
Refrain
Al - le - lu - ia! Al - le - lu - ia!

WORDS: Attrib. to Jean Tisserand, 15th century; transl. Ruth C. Duck, 1995;
copyright © 1996 The Pilgrim Press

MUSIC: O FILII ET FILIAE, *Airs sur les hymnes sacrez,* 1623

ALTERNATE TUNE: GELOBT SEI GOTT

25 O Sons and Daughters, Sing Your Praise

O sons and daughters, sing your praise
on this most holy day of days.
For Christ from death to life is raised.
Alleluia! Alleluia!

When Magdalene and Salome
and Mary went where Jesus lay,
they found the stone was rolled away.
Alleluia! Alleluia!

An angel greeted them and said,
"The Christ is risen from the dead.
To Galilee he goes ahead."
Alleluia! Alleluia!

Among disciples Christ appeared.
"My peace be with you," was his word,
but Thomas doubted when he heard.
Alleluia! Alleluia!

"Come, Thomas, see my hands and side.
I am the one they crucified."
"My God, my Savior!" Thomas cried.
Alleluia! Alleluia!

"How blest are those who do not see
yet place their faith and trust in me.
They shall have life eternally."
Alleluia! Alleluia!

Repeat stanza 1.

Words: Attrib. Jean Tisserand (15th century); transl. Ruth C. Duck, 1995; copyright © 1996 The Pilgrim Press
Meter: 8.8.8. with alleluias

26 O Spirit, Spring of Hidden Pow'r

Unison
Gm A°/G E♭M7 Dm7 Gm
1 O Spir - it, spring of hid - den pow'r that hal - lows day and night: You
2 O Spir - it of the ho - ly cry for hu - man dig - ni - ty, you
3 O Spir - it of un - dy - ing life, O breath with - in our breath: You
E♭ B♭ E♭ F Gm
are the force that prods the flow'r through pave - ment toward the light. You
are the pride of head held high be - fore all big - ot - ry. Your
are the wit - ness in our strife that love sur - pass - es death. You
B♭ Dm Cm F7 B♭ E♭ A°/C Dm7
are the song that brings re - lease; in pris - on cell you do not cease.
rhy - thm rous - es wea - ry feet to move to free - dom's stead - y beat.
are the gift that we de - sire; a - noint our heads with tongues of fire.
Refrain
Gm F/A B♭ E♭ Dm7 Gm Cm/E♭ Dm Gm
Spring of pow'r, fire of love, giv - er of life: come, re - new - ing Spir - it, come.

WORDS: Ruth C. Duck, 1994; copyright © 1996 The Pilgrim Press
MUSIC: UNE JEUNE PUCELLE, French folk melody, 16th century; harm. Jonathan McNair, 1993; copyright © 1993 The Pilgrim Press

26 O Spirit, Spring of Hidden Pow'r

O Spirit, spring of hidden pow'r
that hallows day and night:
You are the force that prods the flow'r
through pavement toward the light.
You are the song that brings release;
in prison cell you do not cease.

Refrain:
Spring of pow'r, fire of love, giver of life:
come, renewing Spirit, come.

O Spirit of the holy cry
for human dignity,
you are the pride of head held high
before all bigotry.
Your rhythm rouses weary feet
to move to freedom's steady beat.

Refrain:
Spring of pow'r, fire of love, giver of life:
come, renewing Spirit, come.

O Spirit of undying life,
O breath within our breath:
You are the witness in our strife
that love surpasses death.
You are the gift that we desire;
anoint our heads with tongues of fire.

Refrain:
Spring of pow'r, fire of love, giver of life:
come, renewing Spirit, come.

Words: Ruth C. Duck, 1994; copyright © 1996 The Pilgrim Press
Meter: 8.6.8.6.8.8. with refrain

27 We Praise You, God, for Women

1 We praise you, God, for wom - en who lived be - fore their time,
2 We praise you, God, for wom - en who cham-pioned free-dom's cause:
3 We praise you God, for wom - en who made your call their choice.
4 We praise you God, for wom - en who ven - tured paths un - known
for proph-ets, priests, and ab - bess - es, for po - ets with their rhyme.
So - journ - er Truth and Ros - a Parks, who chal - lenged e - vil laws.
The church de - nied, but they af - firmed your Spir - it's in - ward voice.
with faith that you had called them there and claimed them as your own.
Great Hil - de - gard of fi - ery tongue, Te - re - sa, tire-less, bold:
They spoke the truth and held their ground, re - sist - ing what was wrong.
They break the bread and bless the cup, though that was man's do - main.
When we lose heart, then bring to mind the cour-age you be - stow.
such wom - en lived with trust in you, and broke tra - di - tion's mold.
They rest - ed on your love and pow'r; their cour - age makes us strong.
Their priest-hood o - pens worlds of grace to heal our grief and pain.
The saints sur-round, a wit - ness cloud to cheer us as we go.

WORDS: Ruth C. Duck, 1993; copyright © 1996 The Pilgrim Press
MUSIC: HILDEGARD OF BINGEN by Joy F. Patterson, 1993; copyright © 1994 Selah Publishing Co., Inc., Kingston, N.Y. 12401.

27 We Praise You, God, for Women

We praise you, God, for women
who lived before their time,
for prophets, priests, and abbesses,
for poets with their rhyme.
Great Hildegard of fiery tongue,
Teresa, tireless, bold:
such women lived with trust in you,
and broke tradition's mold.

We praise you, God, for women
who championed freedom's cause:
Sojourner Truth and Rosa Parks,
who challenged evil laws.
They spoke the truth and held their ground,
resisting what was wrong.
They rested on your love and pow'r;
their courage makes us strong.

We praise you, God, for women
who made your call their choice.
The church denied, but they affirmed
your Spirit's inward voice.
They break the bread and bless the cup,
though that was man's domain.
Their priesthood opens worlds of grace
to heal our grief and pain.

We praise you, God, for women
who ventured paths unknown
with faith that you had called them there
and claimed them as your own.
When we lose heart, then bring to mind
the courage you bestow.
The saints surround, a witness cloud
to cheer us as we go.

Words: Ruth C. Duck, 1993; copyright © 1996 The Pilgrim Press
Meter: 7.6.8.6.8.6.8.6.

28 In Christ Called to Worship

1 In Christ called to wor - ship, we of - fer our praise,
2 In Christ called to bap - tize, we wit - ness to grace,
3 In Christ called to ban - quet, one ta - ble we share,
4 In Christ called to wit - ness, we preach the good news
with thanks for the mer - cies that bless all our days.
and gath - er a peo - ple from each land and race.
a ha - ven of wel - come, a cir - cle of care.
that God loves all peo - ple and frees us to choose.
The Spir - it that search - es the depth of our hearts
In deep, flow - ing wa - ters, we share in Christ's death,
Our mem - bers, one bod - y, par - take in one bread.
By grace may our liv - ing give proof to our praise
gives form to our long - ings, our hopes, and our arts.
then, ris - ing to new life, give thanks with each breath.
One cup of thanks - giv - ing pro - claims Christ, our head.
in cost - ly com - pas - sion re - flect - ing Christ's ways.

WORDS: Ruth C. Duck, 1995; copyright © 1996 The Pilgrim Press
MUSIC: ST. DENIO, Adapt. from a Welsh ballad in John Roberts's *Caniadaeth y Cysegr,* 1839
ALTERNATE TUNE: FOUNDATION

28 In Christ Called to Worship

In Christ called to worship, we offer our praise,
with thanks for the mercies that bless all our days.
The Spirit that searches the depth of our hearts
gives form to our longings, our hopes, and our arts.

In Christ called to baptize, we witness to grace,
and gather a people from each land and race.
In deep, flowing waters, we share in Christ's death,
then, rising to new life, give thanks with each breath.

In Christ called to banquet, one table we share,
a haven of welcome, a circle of care.
Our members, one body, partake in one bread.
One cup of thanksgiving proclaims Christ, our head.

In Christ called to witness, we preach the good news
that God loves all people and frees us to choose.
By grace may our living give proof to our praise
in costly compassion reflecting Christ's ways.

WORDS: Ruth C. Duck, 1995; copyright © 1996 The Pilgrim Press
METER: 11.11.11.11.

29 Faithful God, You Have Been Our Guide

C F G Dm G Dm/F C/E G
1 Faith-ful God, you have been our guide, year by year walk-ing by our side,
2 You have called us to be a light, sign of jus-tice and truth and right.
3 God, what-ev-er the fu-ture holds, keep us faith-ful as life un-folds.
*4 Ho-ly Spir-it, come bless our feast join-ing north and south, west and east.
C F G Dm7 C G C
bless-ing chal-lenge and heal-ing strife, lead-ing us on the way of life.
You have made us a rain-bow sign, col-ors show-ing your peace de-sign.
Write your cov-e-nant on our hearts; send the gifts that your love im-parts.
Bless the gifts on our ta-ble spread: cup of cov-e-nant, liv-ing bread.
Refrain (first time p, second time f)
C C7 F Dm G C F C
Faith-ful God of the liv-ing cov-e-nant, lead us on-ward in this new day.

* St. 4 is optional, for communion Sundays.

WORDS: Ruth C. Duck, 1995; copyright © 1996 The Pilgrim Press
MUSIC: LINSTEAD, Jamaican folk song; adapt. Doreen Potter, 1975;
copyright © 1975 Hope Publishing Co., Carol Stream IL 60188.
All rights reserved. Used by permission.

29 Faithful God, You Have Been Our Guide

Faithful God, you have been our guide,
year by year walking by our side,
blessing challenge and healing strife,
leading us on the way of life.

REFRAIN:
Faithful God of the living covenant,
lead us onward in this new day.

You have called us to be a light,
sign of justice and truth and right.
You have made us a rainbow sign,
colors showing your peace design.

REFRAIN:
Faithful God of the living covenant,
lead us onward in this new day.

God, whatever the future holds,
keep us faithful as life unfolds.
Write your covenant on our hearts;
send the gifts that your love imparts.

REFRAIN:
Faithful God of the living covenant,
lead us onward in this new day.

(FOR COMMUNION SUNDAYS:)

Holy Spirit, come bless our feast
joining north and south, west and east.
Bless the gifts on our table spread:
cup of covenant, living bread.

REFRAIN:
Faithful God of the living covenant,
lead us onward in this new day.

WORDS: Ruth C. Duck, 1995; copyright © 1996 The Pilgrim Press
METER: 8.8.8.8.10.8.

30 God Who Made the Stars of Heaven

Unison
1 God who made the stars of heav - en, God who spread the earth,
2 Liv - ing Christ, the light of na - tions, ra - diant as the sun,
3 Spir - it God, e - quip your peo - ple, all with gifts to share:
4 So may peo - ples praise your great - ness, do your will on earth,
breath of ev' - ry liv - ing be - ing, source of life and birth,
build us up, a grow - ing bod - y; knit your church as one.
mes - sen - gers to speak the gos - pel, min - is - ters of care.
free the cap - tives from their pris - ons, treat the poor with worth.
you have formed us as your peo - ple, led us by your hand.
May our lov - ing be a wit - ness all the world may see.
So may val - leys rise to great - ness, moun - tains be a plain.
So may des - ert, coast, and vil - lage sing new songs to you.
Light of na - tions, shine in us, bright - en ev' - ry land.
Send your Spir - it, bond of peace, source of u - ni - ty.
Come, sur - prise us; change our lives; heal the hearts in pain.
May your Spir - it fill the world, mak - ing all things new.

WORDS: Ruth C. Duck, 1995; copyright © 1996 The Pilgrim Press
MUSIC: THIAN-BENG by I-to Loh, 1996; copyright © 1996 I-to Loh

30 God Who Made the Stars of Heaven

God who made the stars of heaven,
God who spread the earth,
breath of ev'ry living being,
source of life and birth,
you have formed us as your people,
led us by your hand.
Light of nations, shine in us,
brighten ev'ry land.

Living Christ, the light of nations,
radiant as the sun,
build us up, a growing body;
knit your church as one.
May our loving be a witness
all the world may see.
Send your Spirit, bond of peace,
source of unity.

Spirit God, equip your people,
all with gifts to share:
messengers to speak the gospel,
ministers of care.
So may valleys rise to greatness,
mountains be a plain.
Come, surprise us; change our lives;
heal the hearts in pain.

So may peoples praise your greatness,
do your will on earth,
free the captives from their prisons,
treat the poor with worth.
So may desert, coast, and village
sing new songs to you.
May your Spirit fill the world,
making all things new.

WORDS: Ruth C. Duck, 1995; copyright © 1996 The Pilgrim Press
METER: 8.5.8.5.8.5.7.5.

31 With Gifts That Differ by Your Grace

1 With gifts that dif - fer by your grace your Spir - it fits us
2 And yet, be-cause our faith is frail, we bur - y gifts you
3 Come, Spir - it, build your church a - new, that all may do their
all, that Chris - tians in each time and place may
give. A - fraid to risk, a - fraid to fail, we
part, to - geth - er find - ing life in you, di -
an - swer when you call. You strength - en some to take a
are not free to live. At times we use your sa - cred
verse, yet one in heart. So may your peo - ple seek your

Words: Ruth C. Duck, 1995; copyright © 1996 The Pilgrim Press
Music: GIFTS by Arthur G. Clyde, 1997; copyright © 1997 The Pilgrim Press
Alternate Tune: ELLACOMBE

stand, to proph - e - sy or preach, while
gifts for on - ly self - ish ends. Our
will, trans - formed in all our ways. We
oth - ers give with o - pen hand, or heal the sick, or teach.
pur - pose fades, our fo - cus shifts, and con - flict soon at - tends.
of - fer bod - y, mind and skill, a sac - ri - fice of praise.

31 With Gifts That Differ by Your Grace

With gifts that differ by your grace
your Spirit fits us all,
that Christians in each time and place
may answer when you call.
You strengthen some to take a stand,
to prophesy or preach,
while others give with open hand,
or heal the sick, or teach.

And yet, because our faith is frail,
we bury gifts you give.
Afraid to risk, afraid to fail,
we are not free to live.
At times we use your sacred gifts
for only selfish ends.
Our purpose fades, our focus shifts,
and conflict soon attends.

Come, Spirit, build your church anew,
that all may do their part,
together finding life in you,
diverse, yet one in heart.
So may your people seek your will,
transformed in all our ways.
We offer body, mind, and skill,
a sacrifice of praise.

Words: Ruth C. Duck, 1995; copyright © 1996 The Pilgrim Press
Meter: 8.6.8.6.D (CMD)

32 Welcome, Child of the Promise

♩. = 92 - 96
Fine
1 Wel - come, child of the prom - ise,
2 Wel - come, sis - ter or broth - er,
3 Wel - come; share our com - mun - ion.
God's own daugh - ter or son.
young or old, rich or poor.
Eat and drink, take your fill.
Bap - tized, born to one
Since we drink of one
Come and join us in

WORDS: Ruth C. Duck, 1997; copyright © 1997 The Pilgrim Press
MUSIC: DUCK by Carlton R. Young, 1996; copyright © 1997 The Pilgrim Press

bod - y, now in Christ we are one.
Spir - it, we are strang - ers no more.
seek - ing earth re - newed by God's will.
Refrain
Come to the wa - ters, flow - ing, clear,
fount where new life a - bounds.
Live by the Spir - it;
do not fear.
God is here; love sur - rounds.
D.C. al Fine
D.C. al Fine

32 Welcome, Child of the Promise

Welcome, child of the promise,
God's own daughter or son.
Baptized, born to one body,
now in Christ we are one.

REFRAIN:
Come to the waters, flowing, clear,
fount where new life abounds.
Live by the Spirit; do not fear.
God is here; love surrounds.

Welcome, sister or brother,
young or old, rich or poor.
Since we drink of one Spirit,
we are strangers no more.
REFRAIN

Welcome; share our communion.
Eat and drink, take your fill.
Come and join us in seeking
earth renewed by God's will.
REFRAIN

WORDS: Ruth C. Duck, 1997; copyright © 1997 The Pilgrim Press
METER: 7.6.7.6. with refrain

33 Walls Mark Our Bound'ries

Guitar capo on 1st fret (play in G Major)
Unison
A♭ (G) E♭ (D) D♭ (C) A♭ (G)
1 Walls mark our bound'-ries and keep us a - part;
2 Walls make us sure who is in and who's out;
3 Once we were strang - ers, di - vi - ded, a - lone.
D♭ (C) A♭ (G) B♭min (Amin) E♭ (D)
walls keep the world from our eyes and our heart.
walls keep us safe from all ques - tion and doubt,
Hate and dis - trust built a wall stone by stone.
Fmin (Emin) Cmin (Bmin) D♭ (C) A♭ (G)
Ta - bles are round, mak - ing room for one more,
but at a ta - ble in o - pen ex - change
Now at a ta - ble the bread that we share
D♭ (C) A♭/C (G) B♭min (Amin) E♭ (D)
Chorus
wel - com - ing friends we had not known be - fore. So
new ties are formed as our lives re - ar - range. So
joins us to Christ in a cir - cle of care. So

WORDS: Ruth C. Duck, 1994; copyright © 1996 The Pilgrim Press
MUSIC: PENROSE by Jim Strathdee, 1996; copyright © 1997 The Pilgrim Press

A♭ (G)
E♭ (D)
D♭ (C)
A♭ (G)
build us a ta - ble and tear down the wall!
D♭ (C)
A♭/C (G)
B♭min (Amin)
Fmin (Emin)
Christ is our host. There is room
D♭ (C)
E♭ (D)
1,2
A♭ (G)
D♭/A♭ (C)
for us all!
A♭ (G)
E♭7 (D7)
3.
A♭ (G)
all!

33 Walls Mark Our Bound'ries

Walls mark our bound'ries and keep us apart;
walls keep the world from our eyes and our heart.
Tables are round, making room for one more,
welcoming friends we had not known before.

REFRAIN:
So build us a table and tear down the wall!
Christ is our host. There is room for us all!

Walls make us sure who is in and who's out;
walls keep us safe from all question and doubt,
but at a table in open exchange
new ties are formed as our lives rearrange.

REFRAIN:
So build us a table and tear down the wall!
Christ is our host. There is room for us all!

Once we were strangers, divided, alone.
Hate and distrust built a wall stone by stone.
Now at a table the bread that we share
joins us to Christ in a circle of care.

REFRAIN:
So build us a table and tear down the wall!
Christ is our host. There is room for us all!

WORDS: Ruth C. Duck, 1994; copyright © 1996 The Pilgrim Press
METER: 10.10.10.10. with refrain

34 Holy God of Cloud and Flame

♩ = 124
Fine (last time).
ff
1 Ho - ly God of cloud and flame, you feed your sons and daugh - ters.
2 Christ, from crowd - ed cit - y street you bid us share your ta - ble,
3 Spir - it, come and fill each heart, that we may taste and won - der:
Lov - ing, call - ing each by name, you lead us through deep wa - ters.
ask - ing all to come and eat, ig - nor - ing ev' - ry la - bel.
Christ, who loved us from the start, ful - fills our thirst, our hun - ger.
With saints and an - gels
You called us here that
Come, make your church a
7

WORDS: Ruth C. Duck, 1996; copyright © 1996 The Pilgrim Press
MUSIC: SING THE STORY by Carlton R. Young, 1996; copyright © 1997 The Pilgrim Press

we re - joice to praise you, join - ing voice to voice.
night of dread to share your life, your cup, your bread.
sign of care for friends and stran - gers ev' - ry - where.
Refrain
Lov - ing God, Ho - ly One, the earth re - flects your glo - ry.
3
Je - sus Christ, till you come, the church will sing your sto - ry.
D.C. al Fine
D.C. al Fine

34 Holy God of Cloud and Flame

Holy God of cloud and flame,
you feed your sons and daughters.
Loving, calling each by name,
you lead us through deep waters.
With saints and angels we rejoice
to praise you, joining voice to voice.

Refrain:
Loving God, Holy One,
the earth reflects your glory.
Jesus Christ, till you come,
the church will sing your story.

Christ, from crowded city street
you bid us share your table,
asking all to come and eat,
ignoring ev'ry label.
You called us here that night of dread
to share your life, your cup, your bread.
Refrain

Spirit, come and fill each heart,
that we may taste and wonder:
Christ, who loved us from the start,
fulfills our thirst, our hunger.
Come, make your church a sign of care
for friends and strangers ev'rywhere.
Refrain

Words: Ruth C. Duck, 1996; copyright © 1996 The Pilgrim Press
Meter: 7.7.7.7.8.8. with refrain

35 Today We Have Gathered

1 To - day we have gath - ered to wit - ness and bless
2 We pray that the Spir - it will guide you in peace,
3 Praise God, come to meet us and share hu - man life,
two lives joined to - geth - er through vows they pro - fess:
that through chang - ing sea - sons your love may in - crease.
our ho - ly com - pan - ion in joy and in strife.
"To - day and to - mor - row I'll go where you go.
Re - spect one an - oth - er; re - ceive as you give.
May God, who is faith - ful, give grace to us all
Your home shall be my home; your God I shall know."
God's love light your path - way as long as you live.
to go where Christ leads us and an - swer love's call.

WORDS: Ruth C. Duck, 1994; copyright © 1996 The Pilgrim Press
MUSIC: FOUNDATION, early United States melody from Funk's *Genuine Church Music*, 1832
ALTERNATE TUNE: ST. DENIO

35 Today We Have Gathered

Today we have gathered to witness and bless
two lives joined together through vows they profess:
"Today and tomorrow I'll go where you go.
Your home shall be my home; your God I shall know."

We pray that the Spirit will guide you in peace,
that through changing seasons your love may increase.
Respect one another; receive as you give.
God's love light your pathway as long as you live.

Praise God, come to meet us and share human life,
our holy companion in joy and in strife.
May God, who is faithful, give grace to us all
to go where Christ leads us and answer love's call.

Words: Ruth C. Duck, 1994; copyright © 1996 The Pilgrim Press
Meter: 11.11.11.11.

36 Healing River of the Spirit

Unison
1 Heal - ing riv - er of the Spir - it, bathe the wounds that liv - ing brings.
2 Well - spring of the heal - ing Spir - it, stream that flows to bring re - lease,
3 Liv - ing stream that heals the na - tions, make us chan - nels of your pow'r.
Plunge our pain, our sin, our sad - ness deep be - neath your sa - cred springs.
as we gain our selves, our sens - es, may our lives re - flect your peace.
All the world is torn by con - flict; wars are rag - ing at this hour.
Wea - ry from the rest - less search - ing that has lured us from your side,
Grate - ful for the flood that heals us, may your church en - act your grace.
Sav - ing Spir - it, move a - mong us; guide our wind - ing hu - man course,
we dis - cov - er in your pres - ence peace the world can - not pro - vide.
As we meet both friend and strang - er, may we see our Sav - ior's face.
till we find our way to - geth - er, flow - ing home - ward to our Source.

WORDS: Ruth C. Duck, 1994; copyright © 1996 The Pilgrim Press
MUSIC: JOEL by Sally Ann Morris, 1991; copyright © 1997 The Pilgrim Press
ALTERNATE TUNE: BEACH SPRING

36 Healing River of the Spirit

Healing river of the Spirit,
bathe the wounds that living brings.
Plunge our pain, our sin, our sadness
deep beneath your sacred springs.
Weary from the restless searching
that has lured us from your side,
we discover in your presence
peace the world cannot provide.

Wellspring of the healing Spirit,
stream that flows to bring release,
as we gain our selves, our senses,
may our lives reflect your peace.
Grateful for the flood that heals us,
may your church enact your grace.
As we meet both friend and stranger,
may we see our Savior's face.

Living stream that heals the nations,
make us channels of your pow'r.
All the world is torn by conflict;
wars are raging at this hour.
Saving Spirit, move among us,
guide our winding human course,
till we find our way together,
flowing homeward to our Source.

WORDS: Ruth C. Duck, 1994; copyright © 1996 The Pilgrim Press
METER: 8.7.8.7.D

37 When Painful Mem'ries Haunt Each Day

1 When pain - ful mem' - ries haunt each day and dreams dis - turb the night,
2 When dreams at last bring peace and rest, and fear has lost con - trol,
when life is washed with shades of gray and phan - toms fill our sight,
when, tried by strug - gle, we are blessed with right - ful mind and soul,
Christ, stay be - side us and em - brace the child who dwells with - in;
stay close be - side us as be - fore, to guide us all our days.

WORDS: Ruth C. Duck, 1997; copyright © 1997 The Pilgrim Press
MUSIC: MOSHIER by Sally Ann Morris, 1995; copyright © 1995 by G.I.A. Publications, Inc.
ALTERNATE TUNE: KINGSFOLD or CONSOLATION

come, Heal - er, touch our lives with grace; re - store our lives a - gain.
Christ, take the lives that you re - store and fit them for your praise.

37 When Painful Mem'ries Haunt Each Day

When painful mem'ries haunt each day
and dreams disturb the night,
when life is washed with shades of gray
and phantoms fill our sight,
Christ, stay beside us and embrace
the child who dwells within;
come, Healer, touch our lives with grace;
restore our lives again.

When dreams at last bring peace and rest,
and fear has lost control,
when, tried by struggle, we are blessed
with rightful mind and soul,
stay close beside us as before,
to guide us all our days.
Christ, take the lives that you restore
and fit them for your praise.

WORDS: Ruth C. Duck, 1994; copyright © 1996 The Pilgrim Press
METER: 8.6.8.6.D (CMD)

38 When the Winds Rage All Around Us

F Faug B♭Maj7 Gmin7 F/C Dmin
1 When the winds rage all a - round us, shak - ing all that
2 Not our good - ness nor our knowl - edge, our a - chieve - ments
3 When our faith it - self is frag - ile, you are faith - ful
B♭ F F Faug B♭Maj7 Gmin
we hold dear, when the flood of pain en - gulfs us,
nor our art, can sup - port us in the cha - os
with - out fail, send - ing friends to bear your pres - ence
F/C Dmin B♭ Bdim F/C C A/C♯ Dmin
when we feel the grip of fear: We hope in you, O God. We
when our lives are ripped a - part: We hope in you, O God. We
while the storms of change as - sail: We hope in you, O God. We

WORDS: Ruth C. Duck, 1994; copyright © 1996 The Pilgrim Press
MUSIC: WE TRUST IN YOU by Lamont Lenox, 1996; copyright © 1997 The Pilgrim Press

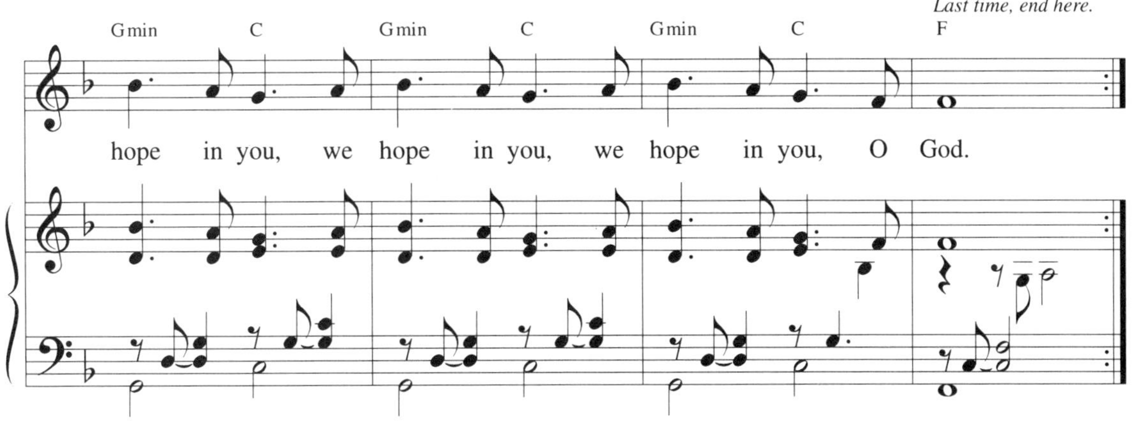
Last time, end here.
Gmin C Gmin C Gmin C F
hope in you, we hope in you, we hope in you, O God.

38 When the Winds Rage All Around Us

When the winds rage all around us,
shaking all that we hold dear,
when the flood of pain engulfs us,
when we feel the grip of fear:
We hope in you, O God.

Not our goodness nor our knowledge,
our achievements nor our art,
can support us in the chaos
when our lives are ripped apart:
We hope in you, O God.

When our faith itself is fragile,
you are faithful without fail,
sending friends to bear your presence
while the storms of change assail:
We hope in you, O God.

WORDS: Ruth C. Duck, 1994; copyright © 1996 The Pilgrim Press
METER: 8.7.8.7.6.

39 Sacred the Body

1 Sa - cred the bod - y God has cre - a -
2 Bod - ies are var - ied, made in all siz -
* 3 Love re - spects per - sons, bod - ies and bound -
4 Ho - ly of ho - lies, God ev - er lov -
ted, tem - ple of Spir - it that dwells deep in -
es, pale, full of col - or, both frag - ile and
'ries. Love does not bat - ter, neg - lect, or a -
ing, make us your tem - ples; in - dwell all we
side. Cher - ish each per - son;
strong. Ho - ly the dif - ference,
buse. Love touch - es gent - ly,
do. May we be care - ful,
nur - ture re - la - tion. Treat flesh as ho -
gift of the Ma - ker, so let us hon -
nev - er co - erc - ing. Love leaves the oth -
ten - der and car - ing, so may our bod -

* *Alternate key signature and accidentals for st. 3 only.*

WORDS: Ruth C. Duck, 1997; copyright © 1997 The Pilgrim Press
MUSIC: TENDERNESS by Colin Gibson, 1992; copyright © 1992 Hope Publishing Co., Carol Stream, IL 60188; all rights reserved; used by permission.

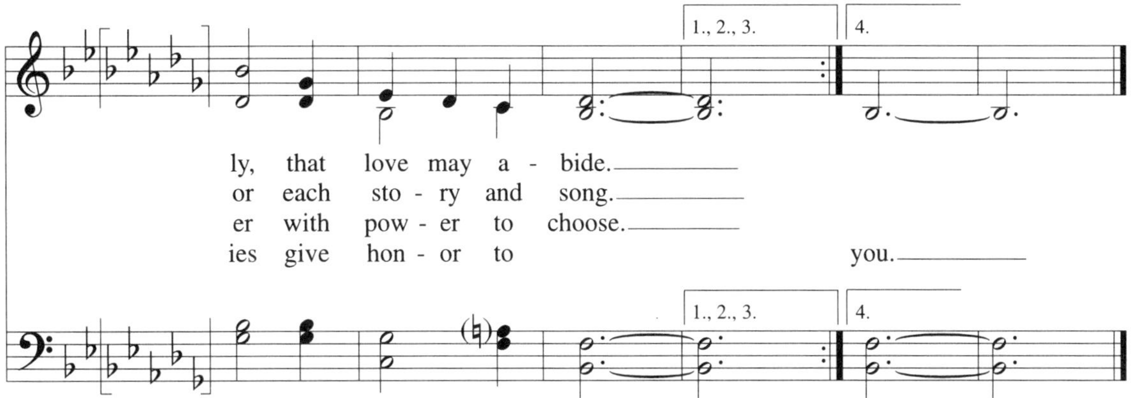
1., 2., 3.
4.
ly, that love may a - bide.
or each sto - ry and song.
er with pow - er to choose.
ies give hon - or to you.
1., 2., 3.
4.

39 Sacred the Body

Sacred the body
God has created,
temple of Spirit that dwells deep inside.
Cherish each person;
nurture relation.
Treat flesh as holy, that love may abide.

Bodies are varied,
made in all sizes,
pale, full of color, both fragile and strong.
Holy the difference,
gift of the Maker,
so let us honor each story and song.

Love respects persons,
bodies and bound'ries.
Love does not batter, neglect, or abuse.
Love touches gently,
never coercing.
Love leaves the other with power to choose.

Holy of holies,
God ever loving,
make us your temples; indwell all we do.
May we be careful,
tender and caring,
so may our bodies give honor to you.

WORDS: Ruth C. Duck, 1997; copyright 1997 The Pilgrim Press
METER: 5.5.10.D

40 God, How Can We Forgive

1 God, how can we for - give when bonds of love are torn?
2 When we have missed the mark, and tears of an-guish flow,
3 Who dares to throw the stone to damn an - oth - er's sin,
How can we rise and start a - new, our trust re - born?
how can you still re - lease our guilt, the debt we owe?
when you, while know - ing all our past, for - give a - gain?
When hu - man lov - ing fails and ev' - ry hope is gone,
The o - cean depth of grace sur - pass - es all our needs.
No more we play the judge, for by your grace we live.
your love gives strength be - yond our own to face the dawn.
A priest who shares our hu - man pain, Christ in - ter - cedes.
As you, O God, for - give our sin, may we for - give.

WORDS: Ruth C. Duck, 1994; copyright © 1996 The Pilgrim Press
MUSIC: LEONI, Traditional Hebrew melody; adapt. Meyer Lyon, 1770

40 God, How Can We Forgive

God, how can we forgive
when bonds of love are torn?
How can we rise and start anew,
our trust reborn?
When human loving fails
and ev'ry hope is gone,
your love gives strength beyond our own
to face the dawn.

When we have missed the mark,
and tears of anguish flow,
how can you still release our guilt,
the debt we owe?
The ocean depth of grace
surpasses all our needs.
A priest who shares our human pain,
Christ intercedes.

Who dares to throw the stone
to damn another's sin,
when you, while knowing all our past,
forgive again?
No more we play the judge,
for by your grace we live.
As you, O God, forgive our sin,
may we forgive.

Words: Ruth C. Duck, 1994; copyright © 1996 The Pilgrim Press
Meter: 6.6.8.4.D

41 Come, Healing Light

1 Come, heal - ing light, ex - pose my pain and ev' - ry need - less ill:
2 Come, sav - ing grace, dis - close my sin, the guilt I hide and store,
3 Come, liv - ing bread, re - veal my need for all I can - not buy.
the gift im - paired or grief un - shared that keeps me from your will,
the trust be - trayed, the good de - layed, the prom - ise I ig - nore,
I spend my days in emp - ty ways that do not sat - is - fy.
for you sur - round our lives with care and heal our bod - y, mind, and soul.
for you for - give be - fore we speak and ask that we in turn for - give.
From north and south and west and east we seek your pres - ence, ho - ly friend.
You an - swer ev' - ry heart - felt prayer; you raise us, make us whole.
Your grace is strong when we are weak and by your word we live.
You wel - come us to share the feast in joy that knows no end.

WORDS: Ruth C. Duck, 1993; copyright © 1996 The Pilgrim Press
MUSIC: WITHOUT WORDS #1 by William P. Rowan, 1993; copyright © 1993 William P. Rowan

41 Come, Healing Light

Come, healing light, expose my pain
and ev'ry needless ill:
the gift impaired or grief unshared
that keeps me from your will,
for you surround our lives with care
and heal our body, mind, and soul.
You answer ev'ry heartfelt prayer;
you raise us, make us whole.

Come, saving grace, disclose my sin,
the guilt I hide and store,
the trust betrayed, the good delayed,
the promise I ignore,
for you forgive before we speak
and ask that we in turn forgive.
Your grace is strong when we are weak
and by your word we live.

Come, living bread, reveal my need
for all I cannot buy.
I spend my days in empty ways
that do not satisfy.
From north and south and west and east
we seek your presence, holy friend.
You welcome us to share the feast
in joy that knows no end.

WORDS: Ruth C. Duck, 1993; copyright 1996 The Pilgrim Press
METER: 8.6.8.6.8.8.8.6.

42 Healing Christ, Shine on Me

Unison
Chorus
Heal - ing Christ, shine on me; make me whole, set me free. Wash me
now in the wa - ters of life. Fill our hearts with your light, with your
4. to
1., 2., 3.
to stanzas
love, burn - ing bright. Come now and calm our strife.
last time only
Fine
now and calm our strife.
1 When we are sick or wor - ried, when we can't face the
2 When we are tired, dis - cour - aged, though we have done our
3 When we are torn, di - vid - ed, blown by the winds of

WORDS: Ruth C. Duck, 1996; copyright © 1996 The Pilgrim Press
MUSIC: ST. OLAF'S by Ruth C. Duck, 1996; copyright © 1997 The Pilgrim Press

day, we need your light to guide us,
best, we need your light to heal us,
strife, we need your lov - ing Spir - it,
to chorus
your word to show the way. Heal - ing
giv - ing us peace and rest. Heal - ing
giv - er of love and life. Heal - ing

42 Healing Christ, Shine on Me

REFRAIN:
Healing Christ, shine on me;
make me whole, set me free.
Wash me now in the waters of life.
Fill our hearts with your light,
with your love, burning bright.
Come now and calm our strife.

When we are sick or worried,
when we can't face the day,
we need your light to guide us,
your word to show the way.
REFRAIN

When we are tired, discouraged,
though we have done our best,
we need your light to heal us,
giving us peace and rest.
REFRAIN

When we are torn, divided,
blown by the winds of strife,
we need your loving Spirit,
giver of peace and life.
REFRAIN

WORDS: Ruth C. Duck, 1996; copyright © 1996 The Pilgrim Press
METER: 7.6.7.6. with refrain

43 As We Meet beside the Lakeshore

1 As we meet be - side the lake-shore, Christ, you beck - on, "Come with me.
2 Can I set to sea like Pe - ter, trem-bling, lost, yet rock - to - be?
3 As I trem - ble by the lake-shore, Christ, you coun - sel, "Do not fear.
Cast your net in deep - er wa-ter; ven - ture toward a far - ther sea."
Can I keep the watch with Ma-ry, faith - ful still while oth - ers flee?
You will catch not fish, but peo-ple; cast your net both far and near."
Calm my fear and fire my cour-age when I hear you call my name.
What po - ten - tial lies with - in me? What ho - ri - zons lie be - fore?
Show me where the need is deep-est and where you would have me go.
Guide me as I jour - ney on-ward, grow - ing as I own your claim.
Stead - y me to trust your Spir - it, wind who blows my boat from shore.
Give me faith to risk and fol-low, leav - ing eve - ry-thing I know.

WORDS: Ruth C. Duck, 1996; copyright © 1996 The Pilgrim Press

MUSIC: ABBOT'S LEIGH by Cyril V. Taylor, 1941; copyright © 1942.
Renewal 1970 Hope Publishing Co., Carol Stream, IL 60188. All rights reserved.
Used by permission.

ALTERNATE TUNE: JEFFERSON

43 As We Meet beside the Lakeshore

As we meet beside the lakeshore,
Christ, you beckon, "Come with me.
Cast your net in deeper water;
venture toward a farther sea."
Calm my fear and fire my courage
when I hear you call my name.
Guide me as I journey onward,
growing as I own your claim.

Can I set to sea like Peter,
trembling, lost, yet rock-to-be?
Can I keep the watch with Mary,
faithful still while others flee?
What potential lies within me?
What horizons lie before?
Steady me to trust your Spirit,
wind who blows my boat from shore.

As I tremble by the lakeshore,
Christ, you counsel, "Do not fear.
You will catch not fish, but people;
cast your net both far and near."
Show me where the need is deepest
and where you would have me go.
Give me faith to risk and follow,
leaving everything I know.

Words: Ruth C. Duck, 1996; copyright © 1996 The Pilgrim Press
Meter: 8.7.8.7.D

44 Twelve Baskets Left Over!

F
B♭
F
1 Twelve bas - kets left o - ver! The great crowd is fed.
(2) bas - kets left o - ver! Our barns bulge with grain.
(3) bas - kets left o - ver, much more than we need!
Gm
C
From few loaves and fish - es a ban - quet is spread.
Why must ten - der chil - dren know hun - ger and pain?
O Christ, name our doubt, our ex - cus - es, our greed.
Am7
Dm7
B♭
F
The needs are so great, our re - sourc - es so small,
God gives us e - nough if we on - ly will share,
Then teach us to trust you each day that we live,
1., 2. Am
Dm7
B♭
Gm7
C
but Christ breaks and bles - ses e - nough for us all.
like Christ, mak - ing just - ice and liv - ing with care. 2 Twelve
to 3 Twelve

WORDS: Ruth C. Duck, 1993; copyright © 1996 The Pilgrim Press
MUSIC: ANDERSON by Jim Strathdee, 1996; copyright © 1997 The Pilgrim Press
ALTERNATE TUNE: ST. DENIO

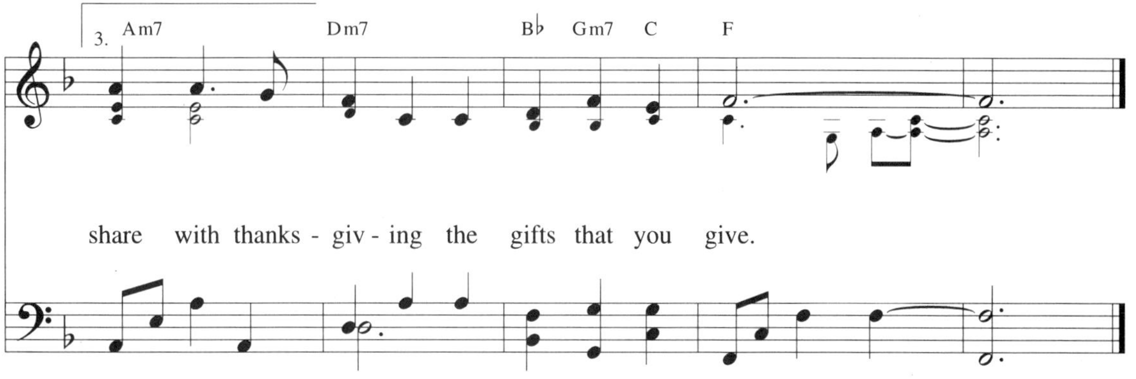
3.
Am7
Dm7
B♭
Gm7
C
F
share with thanks - giv - ing the gifts that you give.

44 Twelve Baskets Left Over!

Twelve baskets left over! The great crowd is fed.
From few loaves and fishes a banquet is spread.
The needs are so great, our resources so small,
but Christ breaks and blesses enough for us all.

Twelve baskets left over! Our barns bulge with grain.
Why must tender children know hunger and pain?
God gives us enough if we only will share,
like Christ, making justice and living with care.

Twelve baskets left over, much more than we need!
O Christ, name our doubt, our excuses, our greed.
Then teach us to trust you each day that we live,
to share with thanksgiving the gifts that you give.

WORDS: Ruth C. Duck, 1993; copyright © 1996 The Pilgrim Press
METER: 11.11.11.11.

45 In Such a Time As This

♩ = 52-54
1 In such a time as this, when crisis claims our best, do we betray you with a kiss or do we meet the test?
2 Was it your holy hand that led us to this place where we must choose to take a stand or flee the task we face?
3 For here the faint of heart fall silent, gripped by fear; they dare no loss to do their part to dry the victim's tear.
4 But others fast and pray and summon all their pow'r; they search for justice, come what may, and speak in danger's hour.
5 Strong Spirit, make us bold to risk for what is right; enflame the faithful as of old with passion, truth, and light.
1., 2., 3., 4.
5.
(last time)

WORDS: Ruth C. Duck, 1996; copyright © 1996 The Pilgrim Press
MUSIC: ROSEMARY by Carlton R. Young, 1996; copyright © 1997 The Pilgrim Press
ALTERNATE TUNE: ST. MICHAEL

45 In Such a Time As This

In such a time as this,
when crisis claims our best,
do we betray you with a kiss
or do we meet the test?

Was it your holy hand
that led us to this place
where we must choose to take a stand
or flee the task we face?

For here the faint of heart
fall silent, gripped by fear;
they dare no loss to do their part
to dry the victim's tear.

But others fast and pray
and summon all their pow'r;
they search for justice, come what may,
and speak in danger's hour.

Strong Spirit, make us bold
to risk for what is right;
enflame the faithful as of old
with passion, truth, and light.

Words: Ruth C. Duck, 1996; copyright © 1996 The Pilgrim Press
Meter: 6.6.8.6. (SM)

46 Holy Wisdom, Lamp of Learning

1 Ho-ly Wis-dom, lamp of learn - ing, bless the light that rea-son lends.
2 Vine of truth, in you we flour - ish; by your grace we learn and grow.
3 Ho-ly God, the hope of na - tions, tune us toward your right-eous will,
Teach us judg-ment as we kin - dle sparks of thought your Spir - it sends.
May the word of Christ a - mong us shape our life, our search to know.
as the sym-pho-ny of a - ges claims our best, our fin - est skill.
Sanc-ti - fy our search for knowl - edge and the truth that sets us free.
Joined to Christ in liv-ing, dy - ing, may we help the church con - vey
Shape our search for peace and jus - tice through pro - phet-ic deed and word.
Come, il - lu - mine mind and spir - it joined in deep-est u - ni - ty.
wit-ness to the sav-ing gos - pel, bear-ing fruit of faith to - day.
Christ, con-duct us, set our rhy - thm, that God's praise be ev - er heard.

WORDS: Ruth C. Duck, 1995; copyright © 1996 The Pilgrim Press
MUSIC: BEACH SPRING, *The Sacred Harp*, 1844; harm. *The New Century Hymnal*, 1992; copyright © 1992 The Pilgrim Press
ALTERNATE TUNE: HYFRYDOL

46 Holy Wisdom, Lamp of Learning

Holy Wisdom, lamp of learning,
bless the light that reason lends.
Teach us judgment as we kindle
sparks of thought your Spirit sends.
Sanctify our search for knowledge
and the truth that sets us free.
Come, illumine mind and spirit
joined in deepest unity.

Vine of truth, in you we flourish;
by your grace we learn and grow.
May the word of Christ among us
shape our life, our search to know.
Joined to Christ in living, dying,
may we help the church convey
witness to the saving gospel,
bearing fruit of faith today.

Holy God, the hope of nations,
tune us toward your righteous will,
as the symphony of ages
claims our best, our finest skill.
Shape our search for peace and justice
through prophetic deed and word.
Christ, conduct us, set our rhythm,
that God's praise be ever heard.

WORDS: Ruth C. Duck, 1995; copyright © 1996 The Pilgrim Press
METER: 8.7.8.7.D

47 Pray for a World

(May be sung in 2 parts using the treble clef notes.
Small notes at beginning and end may be hummed.)
1 Pray for a world where ev - 'ry child finds wel - come in a shel - tered place, where love is ten - der, un - de - filed, and firm - ness in - ter - twines with grace.
2 Pray for a world where pas - sion's fire burns not in force or care - less lust, where God's good gift of deep de - sire is safe in arms of faith and trust.
3 Pray for a na - tion just and fair that seeks the wel - fare of us all, where lead - ers guide with pru - dent care to nur - ture life for great and small.
4 Pray for a world where all have voice and none will bat - ter, rape, a - buse. Till then, may all have right - ful choice and pray for wis - dom as they choose.

WORDS: Ruth C. Duck, 1996; copyright © 1996 The Pilgrim Press
MUSIC: CHILDREN by Arthur G. Clyde, 1997; copyright © 1997 The Pilgrim Press
ALTERNATE TUNE: CANONBURY

47 Pray for a World

Pray for a world where ev'ry child
finds welcome in a sheltered place,
where love is tender, undefiled,
and firmness intertwines with grace.

Pray for a world where passion's fire
burns not in force or careless lust,
where God's good gift of deep desire
is safe in arms of faith and trust.

Pray for a nation just and fair
that seeks the welfare of us all,
where leaders guide with prudent care
to nurture life for great and small.

Pray for a world where all have voice
and none will batter, rape, abuse.
Till then, may all have rightful choice
and pray for wisdom as they choose.

WORDS: Ruth C. Duck, 1996 copyright © 1996 The Pilgrim Press
METER: 8.8.8.8. (LM)

48 We Have Labored, and We Have Baked the Bread

Refrain Unison
We have la-bored, and we have baked the bread. We have wo-ven cloth; we have nur-tured life. Now we're weav-ing a new cre-a-tion, too. Praise, O God, all praise to you!
Last time, end.
1 God of sim-ple, com-mon things, God of cloth and bread, help us mend our tat-tered lives; Spir-it be the thread.
2 As we change our dai-ly lives, jus-tice is our call: saf-er homes and cit-y streets, bread and drink for all.
3 Weave our frayed and var-ied strands, shap-ing one de-sign. May our col-ors rich-ly blend, as our lives en-twine.
4 Clothed in wis-dom, may we live robed in love and praise. May our la-bor turn to joy, as we learn your ways.

WORDS: Ruth C. Duck, 1993; copyright © 1996 The Pilgrim Press
MUSIC: RE-IMAGINING by Donna Kasbohm, 1996; copyright © 1997 The Pilgrim Press

48 We Have Labored, and We Have Baked the Bread

Refrain:
We have labored, and we have baked the bread.
We have woven cloth; we have nurtured life.
Now we're weaving a new creation, too.
Praise, O God, all praise to you!

God of simple, common things,
God of cloth and bread,
help us mend our tattered lives;
Spirit be the thread.
Refrain

As we change our daily lives,
justice is our call:
safer homes and city streets,
bread and drink for all.
Refrain

Weave our frayed and varied strands,
shaping one design.
May our colors richly blend,
as our lives entwine.
Refrain

Clothed in wisdom, may we live
robed in love and praise.
May our labor turn to joy,
as we learn your ways.
Refrain

Words: Ruth C. Duck, 1993; copyright © 1996 The Pilgrim Press
Meter: 7.5.7.5. with refrain

Stories about the Songs and Hymns by Ruth Duck

1 A tune by Lamont Lenox, a Chicago-area gospel musician who is music coordinator for the Greater Holy Temple Church of God in Christ and minister of music at the New Heritage Christian Center, inspired the text *God, Our God, Majestic Creator*. The tune communicated both intimacy and reverent praise, so I decided to paraphrase Psalm 8, which expresses similar feelings, given Lenox's love for worship songs based on the Psalms. A chord progression on Lenox's new electronic keyboard inspired the tune.

2 While reading Psalm 23 devotionally, I noticed a footnote in the New Revised Standard Version of the Bible: "Waters of rest" is an alternative translation for "still waters." I also noticed the words "[God] makes me lie down." These words assure us that it is not the Holy One who spurs us on to ceaseless work and activity, for our loving Shepherd wants us to rest, especially in times of distress. This new insight inspired *Shepherd of My Soul*. The tune I originally used is LE P'ING, a beautiful Chinese melody. Lamont Lenox chose this text for a traditional gospel setting and added music for a chorus.

3 I heard John Bell's haunting tune INCARNATION when I worshiped at the Iona Abbey in Scotland in August 1994. A few days later I visited five-thousand-year-old cave tombs near Avebury, England. Reflecting on this ancient search for the meaning of life and death brought to mind Psalm 90, which contrasts God's eternal being with the fleeting nature of human life. With Bell's tune still ringing in my years, I wrote a paraphrase of the psalm, *Wildflowers Bloom and Fade,* on the plane returning to Chicago. Bell is a member of the Wild Goose Worship Group of the Iona Community and a talented and prolific composer.

4 I wrote *You Gave My Heart New Songs of Praise* for the ordination of Ruth Ann Krymkowski, pastor of two United Church of Christ congregations. She had asked for a hymn using the tune AZMON and based on Psalm 40, which expresses her sense of being called to share the love of God with others. Later, Lamont Lenox provided a lively contemporary tune and chorus. Krymkowski, who experienced a renewal of her faith through her membership at Bethel–Bethany UCC in Milwaukee when I was pastor, calls herself "Rev. Ruth #2."

5 I wrote *God Is at Work in Life* as an act of hope in November 1993, to affirm God's presence during a challenging and painful time in my life. I do not believe that God causes our suffering, though we often hurt one another. God never gives up on us, but ceaselessly labors to bring about the best from the wreckage we create. Students of process thought will recognize in this hymn the influence of Alfred North Whitehead, who said, "God's nature is best conceived . . . as a tender care that nothing be lost. [God's judgment of the world] is the judgment of a tenderness . . . which uses that which in the temporal world is mere wreckage."[1] Yet almost every line paraphrases Scripture, particularly Romans 8 and Psalm 30. I appreciate the sense of hope and newness in the jazz setting by Carlton Young, well-known professor, editor, composer, and conductor.

6 I wrote *Creator of All Time and Space* for the retirement party of three Garrett–Evangelical Theological Seminary colleagues, James Ashbrook, Walter Cason, and Dick Tholin. The original text reflected their commitments as Christians and scholars, though revision was necessary to unify the hymn for general use. As a college student I went through a brief

1. *Process and Reality* (New York: The Free Press, 1929, 1957), 408.

period of doubting the existence of God, but the complex miracles of the human brain and genetic encoding—a central part of Ashbrook's work—were reasons I came to affirm God's working through all of life.

7 In my sophomore Bible class at Rhodes College in Memphis, I learned about Lady Wisdom, an intriguing image of God found in Proverbs, Matthew, 1 Corinthians, and literature between the testaments. As Elizabeth A. Johnson has shown in *She Who Is,* one can express a trinitarian theology based on scriptural Wisdom images. *Come and Seek the Ways of Wisdom* attempts to do just that. Given the deep scriptural roots of this image, the furor in the early 1990s around the use of Sophia imagery for God was perplexing; Sophia is simply the biblical Greek word for Wisdom. Donna Kasbohm, a composer from the Twin Cities, wrote this engaging tune for the November 1994 Re-Imagining gathering. Her musical and liturgical gifts also enrich Wisdom Ways (a spiritual center at the College of St. Catherine and St. Paul) and the Church of St. William, Fridley, Minnesota, as well as the Re-Imagining songbook, *Bring the Feast.*

8 I wrote *Like a Pleading Widow* in August 1995 after hearing a sermon by David Owens, senior pastor of First Congregational UCC, Wilmette, Illinois, where I am a member. By casting God in the role of the woman who persistently presses for justice, he provided an interpretation of the parable of the insistent widow that was new to me. Stanza 2 alludes to a poem by Edwin Markham (1852–1940), a well-loved Disciples of Christ poet, as well as to Francis Thompson's poem "The Hound of Heaven." This new interpretation of the parable suggests that God seeks us, above all, in the faces of human suffering that call us to do justice without delay.

9 When my colleague Barbara Troxell celebrated her sixtieth birthday in 1995, her sister asked for letters and poetry for a scrapbook. Troxell, who teaches spiritual formation at Garrett–Evangelical Theological Seminary, speaks often of Sabbath. She had recently told me that the theme of rest was becoming important to her. So, having done a computer search for all uses of the word "rest" in Scripture, I wrote *Take My Yoke upon You* with gratitude for Barbara's witness to the importance of turning toward God in our busy lives and for TACOMA, a beautiful tune I had just encountered by Daniel Charles Damon, also a friend of Troxell. Damon is pastor of First United Methodist Church in Point Richmond, California, and a doctoral student in theology and music composition at the Graduate Theological Union in Berkeley.

10 *Spirit, Open My Heart* grew out of my own spiritual journey and emerged as part of my discipline of writing hymns each Sunday whenever possible. The hectic pace and challenging diversity of modern life, as well as our woundedness, can make it difficult to remain vulnerable to our emotions and to the humanness of other people. This text, set to the beautiful Irish tune WILD MOUNTAIN THYME, is a prayer that the Spirit may help us be open to the joys and pains of being human together.

11 I wrote both *God of Wisdom, God of Grace* and *Your Glory, O God, in Christ* (13) for a 1996 meeting of the North Central Jurisdiction of the United Methodist Fellowship for Worship, Music, and Other Arts. The theme of the event was "Reflections," centering on Christ as a reflection of God's glory and the church as a reflection of Christ. This was a hard text to write. I imagined mirrors and reflecting pools and meditated on relevant Scriptures (such as 2 Cor. 4:12–18; Heb. 1:1–14; Col. 1:15–20), yet my words were ever inadequate to what I saw in my mind's eye. Ultimately, the planning committee chose *Your Glory, O God.* Several months later I found that the images in the present first stanza of *God of Wisdom, God of Grace* came close to expressing what I had imagined.

12 *In the Dawn of the Ages* is a revision of a text I wrote in 1973 for one of the first Christian feminist liturgies, which was held in Philadelphia. It was first published in *Because We Are One People,* a collection of inclusive-language hymns published by the Ecumenical Women's Center in 1974. Because the text was originally more a parody than a song for congregational worship, I have long wanted to revise it. I finally did so for this volume.

13 *Your Glory, O God.* See *God of Wisdom, God of Grace* (11) to learn about the process for writing this text. Carlton Young's graceful tune GOD'S IMAGE prayerfully complements the text. Young was the editor of both *The Methodist Hymnal* of 1966 and *The United Methodist Hymnal* of 1989.

14 *Glory to God, and Peace on Earth!* is a free paraphrase of the Gloria in Excelsis, originally inspired by a tune by Hal McSwain Jr. I unearthed and revised the text in hopes of seeking a contemporary jazz setting from one of the African American musicians suggested by L. Stanley Davis. When I heard Lamont Lenox play a jazz arrangement of another song, I knew he was the one to set this text. His energetic musical setting to this inclusive-language paraphrase gives contemporary freshness to an ancient text.

15 Brent Stratten, a member of the committee that developed the *Chalice Hymnal,* composed TAFT STREET for use with Thomas Troeger's text "How Long, O Lord, How Long?" in the hymnal. Its feeling of gentle trust moved me to write the text *We Thank You, God, for Prayer.* It is fitting that the text speaks of prayer with images of God as both "mother" and "father," since Stratten and I have often discussed the language of prayer and praise. I was pleased how the Scripture images from Luke 11:11–13 and Isaiah 49:15–16 complement each other. Stratten is currently the organist/choirmaster at Brite Divinity School of Texas Christian University.

16 Given the context of racism in the United States and the frequent negative connotation of darkness in Scripture and tradition, Christian worship should lift up positive aspects of darkness. *Blessed Darkness* was not so much a conscious attempt to address this issue as a gift of text and tune from some deeper source of inspiration. Thus, I see this song as a gift from the darkness of unknowing.

17 The book *She Who Is* by Elizabeth A. Johnson encourages using feminine imagery for God to complement traditions that focus on masculine images. It inspired the text *I Reflect the Image of the Maker.* Constant use of masculine imagery for God makes it difficult for women to experience what it means to be made in the divine image. This simple text, with a reverent tune by Donna Kasbohm, celebrates the divine image in all people and praises the Creator.

18 Ironically, the first draft of *We Thank You, God, for Sunday* was written on a high mountain peak in the Green River area of the Wind River Mountains of Wyoming. On this beautiful sunlit August Sunday, I thought of Christians worshiping around the world, and found myself thanking God for the church's day of resurrection and praise.

19 The text *Here at Jordan's River* grew out of a classroom situation in which several Euro-American students and I were challenged to reflect upon assumptions we make based on our privilege in U.S. society. It is difficult for those with privilege to comprehend the pervasiveness of racism in ourselves and society. Sometimes when challenged we respond with defensiveness or guilt; but our vocation as Christians is to conversion—true change in hearts and lives. Luke's account of John the Baptist's ministry reminds us that none of us can trust inherited privilege, but that baptism is entry into a new reality based on God's grace that calls for conversion.

20 I wrote *You Shall Draw with Gladness* for Judith Lane Chatfield's installation as pastor at the United Church of Christ in LaSalle, Illinois, on December 11, 1994. It was a joyous celebration shared with the congregation, Judy's partner Don Chatfield, UCC pastor and songwriter Jim Manley, and hymnwriter and theologian Brian Wren. The song is my personal reflection and response to two of the day's lectionary passages, Isaiah 12:2–6 and Luke 3:7–16.

21 *O Word Made Flesh among Us* was written for our family Christmas letter of 1996, as well as for a staff-faculty-administration Christmas party. As I reflected on gaps in Christmas hymnody, it appeared that few hymns connect the incarnation of God in Christ with embodied human reality. The image connecting the wood of the manger to the wood of the cross came as a surprise that I resisted. Yet I realized that the cross is part of the way Jesus shared our human life, and thus is an essential part of an incarnational Christmas hymn.

22 When Art Clyde requested a new Epiphany hymn for this volume, I welcomed the idea, since that feast has long fascinated me. I had also wanted to collaborate on a song with Osvaldo D. Vena, who teaches New Testament at Garrett–ETS. We brainstormed together on ideas for a text that would provide an alternative to the usual emphasis on the Magi. The resulting text, *Not in Grand Estate*, demonstrates our common grounding in Scripture and in liberation theology. The song was introduced with Vena's engaging new tune at the Garrett–ETS lecture hour in March 1997.

23 I love to teach a course called "Worship and the Arts." It features regular hands-on exercises in various forms of art, in which I participate with the students. The assignment was to respond artistically to John 12:1–7. I chose to write the text *When Mary Bathed Our Savior's Feet*. It came very easily (to the tune ST. FLAVIAN) after a class meditation on the passage. I shared the text with Brent Stratten, who wrote a moving tune to complement it.

24 At a hymn festival at the Hymn Society in the U.S. and Canada, Carl Daw's new text on the crucifixion, "How Shallow Former Shadows Seem," moved me. Speaking to Daw after the festival, I remarked that I would be very old before I could write a text about the crucifixion. Later I realized I could write a text asking questions about the cross and redemption. Though questions form the first two stanzas of *How Could a God Whose Name Is Love*, I end by affirming that God does not will violent death, but has compassion for all who suffer.

25 *O Sons and Daughters, Sing Your Praise* is my translation for the *Chalice Hymnal* of the Latin text. "O filii et filiae" written by Jean Tisserand in the fifteenth century. As English-language hymnal committees seek to provide contemporary and inclusive-language versions of hymns not originally in English, new translations are often a good alternative.

Returning to the Latin text provided a bonus: translations of "O filii et filiae" with which I was familiar omit the stanzas about the women who visited the tomb.

26 One day, as part of my regular hymn-writing discipline, I decided to write a new hymn for Pentecost. After brainstorming for fresh ideas, I chose to emphasize the way the Spirit prods us toward life and justice in the face of death and injustice. I thought of characters from Toni Morrison's *Beloved* and Zora Neale Hurston's *Their Eyes Were Watching God* who affirm life despite everything, and recalled the faithful witness of Nelson Mandela. *O Spirit, Spring of Hidden Power* was the result. This song can be very effectively accompanied by drum beat only.

27 At the request of Beverly Dale, director of the Christian Association at the University of Pennsylvania, where I was campus ministry intern from 1973 to 1974, I wrote *We Praise You, God, for Women* for the 1994 Philadelphia celebration of the twentieth anniversary of the first ordination of women to priesthood in the Episcopal Church. Although the third stanza highlights the occasion, I wrote a hymn honoring courageous women throughout church history. Joy Patterson's tune, aptly named HILDEGARD OF BINGEN, serves the text well. Patterson, whose collected hymn texts and tunes appear in *Come, You People of the Promise* (Carol Stream, Ill. Hope Publishing Company, 1994) and in several denominational hymnals, is a Presbyterian from Wausau, Wisconsin.

28 I wrote *In Christ Called to Worship* at the request of Anita Stauffer, once a classmate at the University of Notre Dame, for the July 1997 meeting of the Lutheran World Federation in Hong Kong. I changed the first line, originally "In Christ called to baptize," because the hymn is about the church's ministry of word and sacrament and its mission in the world, not only baptism.

29 In October 1995, Covenant United Methodist Church in Evanston, Illinois, celebrated its 125th anniversary. Through the coordination of Janice Butz, ordained deacon and director of music there, I was commissioned to write *Faithful God, You Have Been Our Guide* for the occasion. Expressing a theology of covenant, it grew out of stories Butz told me about the church's history. She wrote an anthem using the text, which can also be sung to LINSTEAD, a Jamaican tune adapted by Doreen Potter for use with Fred Kaan's text "Let Us Talents and Tongues Employ."

30 After I had completed *In Christ Called to Worship* (28, above), Anita Stauffer asked me to write another hymn for the Lutheran World Federation meeting. I based *God Who Made the Stars of Heaven* on the Federation's mission statement and on Isaiah 42:5–8 and Ephesians 4:1–16, texts for the service when the hymn would be sung. Since the meeting would be in Hong Kong, I used an Asian tune, TOKYO, known to English-speaking Christians as the tune for "Here, O God, Your Servants Gather." Anita sent the text to I-to Loh, music director for the meeting. (Loh, the President of Tainan Theological College and Seminary in Taiwan and project director of *Hymns from the Four Winds*, is internationally known for composing new hymn tunes, as well as collecting and transcribing hymns from all over Asia). I was delighted that he composed a new tune, THIAN-BENG, for my text.

31 The book *Glamorous Powers* by Susan Howatch inspired *With Gifts That Differ by Your Grace*. In this engaging novel, Howatch describes an Anglican priest's struggle to use his gifts to fulfill God's calling, not to impress other people or set himself above them. Indeed, faithfully using the gifts God places within us is one of the greatest challenges of the spiritual journey. Will we bury our gifts, use them for self alone, or employ them as we take our part in building human community and glorifying God?

32 Stanzas 1 and 2 of *Welcome, Child of the Promise* are meant to be sung as candidates and sponsors come forward for baptism; stanza 3 can be sung as the participants return to their seats. Carlton ("Sam") Young is distinguished among today's composers for his ability to create tunes that are singable, memorable, and contemporary (with a touch of jazz). He has encouraged me to write simpler texts, and this one inspired a rock-and-roll beat in him. I hope it will inspire baptismal joy.

33 *Walls Mark Our Bound'ries* was inspired by the paradoxical experience of visiting a church that offered vibrant multicultural worship but was struggling with other forms of diversity. After church a small group discussed whether the church was ready to welcome gay, lesbian, and bisexual people. The service and lunch ended later than usual, while a group of homeless people waited restlessly outside to come in for a meals program. I could not help wondering why they were not sitting at the table with us, and whether even the most welcoming churches embody the welcome of Jesus Christ. As soon as I wrote it, I knew that the text begged for a tune by Jim Strathdee; and two years later, that dream became reality. Jim and Jean Strathdee's ministry of music, with a strong emphasis on social justice and human community, has enlivened United Methodist Churches in California as well as conferences throughout the United States and Canada.

34 *Holy God of Cloud and Flame* could serve as a prayer of Great Thanksgiving before communion, because it includes the classic elements of that prayer. The presider would sing the stanzas; the congregation would sing the chorus, which fills the role of the Sanctus ("Holy, Holy, Holy") and memorial acclamation ("Christ has died; Christ is risen; Christ will come again"). (Words of institution would follow.) Or, the choir could sing it during communion, with the congregation singing the chorus. Again, Sam Young heard an upbeat tune growing out of the joyful contemporary nature of the text.

35 *Today We Have Gathered* was written for the marriage of Shannon Conklin and Jeff Miller, drawing on the texts for the service, Ruth 1:16–17 and Matthew 22:35–40 (the Great Commandment). Shannon and Jeff were students at Garrett–Evangelical Theological Seminary. I worked closely with Shannon on the chapel staff at Garrett–ETS. At present, Jeff and Shannon Conklin-Miller are both United Methodist clergy in the Los Angeles area.

36 I wrote *Healing River of the Spirit* on a Sunday in August 1994, on the Isle of Iona in the Hebrides on the west coast of Scotland. Iona Community founder George MacLeod said that the veil between worlds is thin on that island; certainly Iona has been a center for Christian spirituality for many centuries. My visit there with my partner, John Stoppels, was a healing time for me. One of the emphases of the Iona Community is on healing ministries. Therefore, it seemed fitting to write a hymn about healing during some quiet time that day.

37 A friend who experienced childhood sexual abuse had just completed five years of therapy. She invited persons who had been part of her journey to gather for a ritual celebrating her healing. She invited us all to bring a song, a story, a poem, or some other expression to share as part of the ritual. *When Painful Mem'ries Haunt Each Day,* my contribution, speaks of the healing of memories and reordering of a wounded life through the loving presence of Christ. MOSHIER, a beautiful tune by Sally Ann Morris, a talented composer from Winston-Salem, North Carolina, fits it well. It can also be sung to KINGSFOLD.

38 Both text and tune of *When the Winds Rage All Around Us* give testimony through words and sound to God's unfailing love. Though joyful times may inspire us to praise God, times of loss can move us to learn more deeply that abiding hope comes solely from the presence of God in our pain and joy. Although it may be difficult to feel the divine presence in times of grief and chaos, we can often trace how God's love has been mediated to us by other people who have heard and understood us. I originally wrote the text to Peter Cutts's tune BRIDEGROOM. Lamont Lenox's reflective tune gently affirms God's loving presence.

39 Janet Walton, professor of worship at Union Theological Seminary in New York, called to ask if I knew of a congregational song that spoke to issues of battering and abuse by using Paul's concept of the body as the temple of the Holy Spirit (1 Cor. 3:16–17). Some students planning worship at Union had asked for such a song. I didn't know of existing hymn texts on that theme, but the idea inspired *Sacred the Body*. Writing the text provided healing for my distress over a friend's story of being sexually abused by a religious professional. Thanks to Dr. Walton's students for their inspiration!

40 *God, How Can We Forgive* was born out of my struggle to deal with a deep hurt I had suffered. As it turned out, forgiveness has been a long process, in which I must address human relationships and not only my relationship with God. Still, remembering that we all sin and fall short of the glory of God (Romans 3:23) can help in the process of learning to forgive.

41 Usually collaboration between text-writers and composers begins with the text, which inspires a fitting tune. At a hymn-writing workshop, composer Bill Rowan offered his tune WITHOUT WORDS #1 to text-writers, asking why a tune couldn't inspire a text. Indeed, at times the quality of a tune inspires me to write a text; Rowan's tune inspired the text *Come, Healing Light*. Rowan, whose compositions appear in many hymnals, is director of music ministries at St. Mary Cathedral in Lansing, Michigan.

42 After completing my first hymn collection, *Dancing in the Universe* (Chicago: G.I.A., 1992), I experienced writer's block. To spur my creativity, I signed up for a hymn-writing workshop at St. Olaf's College sponsored by the Hymn Society. Although I was not able to follow the assignment of writing a text based on the story of the man born blind (John 9), *Healing Christ, Shine on Me* came to me as a general song about healing. The tune sounded like gospel music to me, but Art Clyde may be more correct in calling it country-western style.

43 I wrote *As We Meet beside the Lakeshore* for the Garrett–Evangelical Theological Seminary spiritual life retreat in September 1996. While writing, I thought of people whom we would welcome to the seminary through the retreat, many of whom have left behind successful careers to follow their calling. Again and again, faithful Christians, lay and clergy, must make the choice to follow Jesus, leaving behind what is past.

44 At a workshop in Toronto, Pamela Moeller, author of *Kinesthetic Homiletic*, led us in bodily meditation on the story of the feeding of the thousands. Then she invited us to share our experiences in small groups. My long-time friend UCC pastor Al Krass was moved to remark that there are enough resources for everyone to have what they need, if we will share. This thought inspired *Twelve Baskets Left Over,* which Krass later used in a Bible study in the Bread for the World newsletter. I am grateful for Jim Strathdee's tune.

45 Rosemary Keller, former faculty member and dean at Garrett–ETS, often quotes these words from the book of Esther: "Perhaps you have come to royal dignity for just such a time as this," spoken by Mordecai to challenge Queen Esther to risk speaking out on behalf of her people. For a book in Keller's honor, I wrote the text *In Such a Time As This,* based on the story of Esther and the call to speak out courageously when we are in a position to make a difference. Young's tune expresses the text's tension perfectly.

46 I was asked to write a hymn in honor of Neal Fisher's fifteenth year as president of Garrett–Evangelical Theological Seminary. In the resulting text, *Holy Wisdom, Lamp of Learning,* I created a poetic version of the seminary's mission statement, which Fisher had led the faculty in forming. The seminary's threefold mission includes evangelical commitment (communicating the gospel), prophetic interaction with society (seeking social justice), and critical and creative reason (faith seeking understanding). I hope that congregations who share this sense of mission will find inspiration in this hymn.

47 The Religious Coalition for Reproductive Choice sponsored worship services in connection with the Democratic and Republican conventions of 1996. They asked me to write a hymn text for these occasions; *Pray for a World* was my response. I wanted to support the importance of reproductive choice, while encouraging serious reflection whenever persons consider whether to end a pregnancy. Arthur Clyde's tune CHILDREN effectively expresses the text's feeling of hope through struggle.

48 *We Have Labored, and We Have Baked the Bread* is one of several texts in this collection that I wrote as a contribution to an event I was unable to attend—this time, a gathering for women's worship at the Parliament of World Religions in September 1993. I wrote the text to fit the service's themes of weaving and bread. It originally spoke of women as bakers of bread and weavers of cloth. Later, the Re-Imagining Community asked me to adapt the text so that it would include men. They used it at one of their gatherings, with an engaging new tune by Donna Kasbohm.

METRICAL INDEX

TUNE INDEX

COMPOSER INDEX

(This list includes the composers of both the new tunes in this collection and other recently composed tunes.)

SCRIPTURE INDEX

Hebrew Bible and Apocrypha

New Testament

SUBJECT INDEX

INDEX OF FIRST LINES